ALPINE ANGLER

A FLY FISHER'S GUIDE TO THE WESTERN WILDERNESS

By John Shewey

Amato *Frank*

PORTLAND

Dedication

To Mom, for turning me loose in the outdoors
at an early age, and to DeAnn for appreciating and
sharing my need to remain loosed on the outdoors.

Acknowledgements

First, I must thank my good friend and original Oregon fishing partner Dewey Weddington, who over the years has endured some brutal trail miles on my heels in pursuit of wilderness lakes (not that those brutal miles will end anytime soon).

Also, a project like this would not be possible without the efficient and timely help of officials from the state fish and game agencies and the U.S. Forest Service. The effort put forth by individuals from these organizations is greatly appreciated.

Finally I offer a special thanks to Tim Blount and to DeAnn Montgomery. Tim will try just about any fishing trip once and may yet suffer some serious psychological disorder as a result of going along with and participating in my fly fishing ideas and adventures. Both he and DeAnn helped a great deal in shooting photos for this book and in offering suggestions on how to proceed.

Cover Photo: John Shewey
All photos by the author except where otherwise noted
Illustrations by Bill Herzog
Book and Cover Design, Chapter Illustration: Kathy Johnson
Printed in Hong Kong

10 9 8 7 6 5 4 3 2 1
ISBN: Softbound 1-878175-98-X, Hardbound 1-878175-99-8

Table of Contents

Introduction 4

Chapter 1: Alpine-Lake Trout and How They Feed 6

Chapter 2: Applying The Structural Approach 10

Chapter 3: Fishing The Hatch: Selective High-Lake Trout 16

Chapter 4: Float Tubing The Alpine Lakes 30

Chapter 5: Before You Go: Getting In Shape For Alpine Travel 34

Chapter 6: Planning Wilderness Fishing Trips 38

Chapter 7: Map and Compass Skills For The Wilderness Traveler 44

Chapter 8: Wilderness Travel Tips 52

Chapter 9: Fishing Alpine Streams 60

Chapter 10: Western Wilderness Areas—An Angler's Guide 64

Introduction

The alpine lakes of America's Western wilderness areas offer some of the finest fly fishing available anywhere. Brook trout, cutthroat, rainbows, golden trout, grayling—take your pick. What's more, the alpine lakes rest quietly amidst some of the most beautiful country to be found, places that defy description and even defy photography to capture their stunning awesomeness in full.

But the alpine lakes come at a price. The quality of your alpine-lake fishing experience is directly proportionate to your willingness to work hard. It is this fact that separates the explorers and adventurers of our fold from those whose fly fishing experience will forever be defined by the famous and crowded Western rivers and by the increasingly popular pay-to-play fish farms being sold to us by those who cater to people not willing to work for their fish and for their solitude.

The alpine lakes do indeed come at a price, but it is a price worth paying over and over. Serious alpine-lake anglers spend hours with their face buried in coffee-stained topo maps, trying to find that potential dream lake. When we find these precious lakes—emerald-colored gems reflecting rugged snow-capped crags and filled with big, hungry trout—we have almost always paid a price in rugged mile after rugged mile on the trail and, more frequently, off the trail on our own routes.

Alpine Angler will show you the skills you need to locate, access and fish the thousands of alpine lakes of the Western wilderness areas. Beyond that, it is up to you: How hard are you willing to work for your fishing and for your solitude? If nothing else, I assure you that if you put the time in—the time to learn and apply the things discussed in this book and the time sweating it out on the trail—you will find exceptional fishing and you will experience exceptional solitude: An increasingly rare combination in today's fly fishing world.

John Shewey,
Bend, Oregon

Ken Hanley photo.

CHAPTER 1
Alpine Lake Trout And How They Feed

If one thing characterizes alpine lakes it is that each has a unique personality. One lake will be stark, deep and barren; yet over the next ridge often lies a shallow, weedy, fertile lake teeming with insects and trout.

One lake supports a healthy population of golden trout that spawn in the tributary streams while another holds nonreproducing rainbows that are planted by helicopter every third or fourth year. Another nearby lake overflows with small, stunted brook trout reproducing at a rate that the food supply cannot really support and still another offers oversized planted cutthroat.

What all these alpine-lake trout have in common is that few are native. Many lakes sustain populations of reproducing trout but generally these populations are of hatchery origin. Virtually every lake in the high country, especially those at 9,000 feet and higher, from Montana and Wyoming to California and Oregon was historically devoid of trout. Most often, trout simply could not reach the alpine lakes because waterfalls on the tributary streams block any upstream migration from larger waters below. Moreover, many lakes experience complete winter kill when severe enough winters occur. For these and other reasons the huge majority of our alpine lakes never had any native trout.

Certainly exceptions can be found: Native cutthroat or bull trout inhabit a precious few alpine lakes. But for the majority of these lakes stocking programs over the years have provided trout populations. Most of these fish plantings have been undertakings of the various fish and game agencies in the different states. Many waters, however, have over the years been stocked by private individuals. In either case, sometimes the introduced trout begin reproducing and sometimes they do not.

Still, where suitable habitat exists even nonreproducing populations can survive for a number of years until a severe winter kills them or until old age takes its toll. Those waters that are heavily fished generally receive the most frequent fish plantings and invariably are the most accessible of the alpine lakes.

We would expect the more fertile lakes to harbor the best trout regardless of whether they reproduce and often this holds true. Frequently, however, a seemingly barren lake will yield surprisingly large trout. Just as often the most fertile of waters prove to be overpopulated with small trout, their growth and size stunted by too much competition for the available food.

Every lake, therefore, holds its own surprises making generalizations rather difficult. Nonetheless, it would be accurate to say that most alpine lakes are relatively infertile when compared to lower elevation trout waters. Weed growth is minimal in many

Many alpine lakes harbor dense populations of small brook trout or cutthroat.

alpine waters; densities of insects and other aquatic trout foods are comparatively low; growing seasons are short as the lakes are only ice-free for two to five months out of the year.

Once in a while you will find those weedy, fertile lakes that by luck of the draw are geographically located on the right exposure and which offer ideal growing conditions for trout (or at least as ideal as can be expected at high elevation). When not overpopulated with stunted fish such lakes can support populations of large, healthy trout.

While shooting photos for this book I happened on a small emerald-colored lake nestled below one of the rugged crags of Idaho's Sawtooth range. Some 9,300 feet above sea level I hardly expected to find 18- and 20-inch cutthroat, yet a handful of these gorgeous trout patrolled the lake's shallow margins. Few in number these fish had ample food to share amongst themselves.

ders, some protruding from the water others under the surface entirely, litter half of the lake's bottom. One side of the lake is timbered rather sparsely with the fallen trees lying waterlogged on the bottom, several of them jutting out from shore. Finally, two tiny streams feed one side of the lake while a single outlet releases water to lakes further down the basin.

This picture could describe thousands of lakes in the Western high country and yet each still holds its own secrets. Wherever the lake though, all these features—from inlets and outlets to shoals and peninsulas—comprise its structural elements. Trout use such structural elements for resting during nonfeeding periods and for escaping potential dangers. They also look for food around structure simply because most of the aquatic organisms in any given lake will be concentrated in these areas.

Because trout rely so heavily on structural elements, the

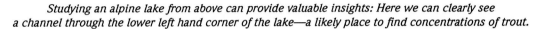

Studying an alpine lake from above can provide valuable insights: Here we can clearly see a channel through the lower left hand corner of the lake—a likely place to find concentrations of trout.

Add another few dozen fish to such a lake and the average size of the trout would probably decline with the added competition for available food.

Indeed that tiny lake offers a valuable lesson to alpine anglers: You can find big trout in abundance in a very fertile, weedy lake but you might find even larger trout—albeit only a handful of them—in a comparatively infertile lake if the number of fish is small enough that all have ample food.

In any event, let's try to paint a picture of a typical alpine lake. Imagine a rather deep lake, its middle a dark bluish-green color, with three sides offering gently sloping shallows and the fourth abruptly meeting a talus slide or a sheer rock face that forms the bottom of a high, steep ridge. Its shoreline irregular in shape this lake includes a peninsula jutting into the lake from one shore, leaving a narrow bay on one side. A few huge boul-

best approach to any alpine lake is to first identify the structures where fish are likely to be found. Having done that you can concentrate your efforts around these structural elements with full confidence that you are fishing the most productive areas of any given lake. We can label this concept the "structural approach."

When identifying the structural elements of any given lake try to give yourself the advantage of elevation. If possible, study the lake from a ridgetop before making the descent. After a long hike you will want nothing more than to get to the lake and dump your pack, but the opportunity to study a lake's features from above, especially with field glasses, is well worth the time. If this is impossible, approach the lake carefully, well back from the shore, studying the structural features before ever assembling a rod.

*From high above we can easily locate
the inlet streams, shoal areas, channels, dropoffs
and other structural elements of this high lake in Oregon.*

To fully appreciate the relationship between stillwater trout and a lake's structural elements, anglers must first understand the behavior of stillwater trout. Trout living in streams can remain relatively stationary and wait for the current to carry food to them, but stillwater trout must go out and find their food. In a super-fertile lake the fish may not have to move very far to find adequate amounts of food but in the typical alpine lake, where insects and other foods are at a premium, trout often wander almost endlessly always on the prowl for whatever edible morsel might be found.

This behavior is usually referred to as "cruising." What's more, trout often establish regular "cruising routes:" They prowl about the lake or a part of the lake following the same general path repeatedly. Significantly, cruising trout tend to look for food near structural elements like shoals, drop-offs, inlets,

Alpine-lake trout spend much of their time cruising along shallows looking for food.

logs, rocks, weeds, overhanging brush, etc. So long as nothing disturbs them these trout will cruise the same circuit over and over, usually straying slightly from the original path with each successive lap.

As important as the strategy of cruising is to alpine-lake trout, they do employ other feeding methods as well. Sometimes trout simply hide under the shade of a fallen log or a submerged boulder remaining motionless until something edible wanders too close. Other times they hold at the mouth of a tributary stream and wait for the currents to wash food into the lake. When the wind blows and blows rather hard trout gather at the leeward side of a lake and eat the insects that have been blown across the lake and deposited en masse near one shoreline. Or they start at one end of the lake and simply swim into the wind near the shore looking for terrestrial insects that have been blown into the water. Finally, when a hatch of some aquatic insect occurs trout concentrate their feeding efforts around that emergence.

Alpine-lake trout use all of these feeding strategies, often in combination or at least switching from one to the other when conditions dictate such changes. For the alpine-lake angler this translates to opportunity: Identify a cruising route and catch that trout; find a sunken log or boulder or a sudden drop-off and maybe find a trout waiting in ambush; during a windy day fish the leeward side; sneak up to a tributary and drift a fly to a waiting trout. In virtually all these scenarios structural elements comprise an integral part of the trout's feeding strategy. Therefore, the strategy you employ for fishing any given alpine lake should revolve around first understanding the way trout feed in these waters and then taking advantage of the fact that structural elements will be a significant ingredient in the trout's feeding method.

Lake structures and trout feeding strategies: 1. High-lake trout will cruise in more or less regular routes (B, D and E) looking for food. 2. Inlets and outlets provide currents that wash food to waiting fish (A and C).
3. Sometimes trout will simply lie in the shadow of a rock or log, resting for a time and taking advantage of any insect that might happen by (F).

CHAPTER 2

Applying The Structural Approach

THE temptation of every angler new to the alpine lakes is to climb up on the nearest shoreline rock and cast toward deep water. In reality this is the last strategy you should employ—at times a valuable ploy but not usually the best choice right off the bat.

Instead, study the shallows: In any alpine lake the shallows, where light penetration is best and where the lake's only weed growth occurs, must be considered a structural element in their own right. This shallow zone in a lake is called the littoral zone which is just a fancy name for shallows with good light penetration and potential for weed growth. The vast majority of aquatic trout foods in any lake live within this littoral zone, which might span four or five feet in depth or might extend 15 or 20 feet or more, depending on the clarity of the water and the extent to which sunlight can penetrate.

The shallows also offer warmer water: Alpine lake trout live in the coldest of lakes with temperatures frequently hovering well below the low- to mid-50s preferred by many salmonids. Because the sun warms the shallows much faster than the deep water, trout show a marked preference for these shallow areas.

In addition to finding warmer water, trout find most of their food in shallower water. Thus alpine-lake trout spend most of their feeding time cruising these areas, especially where cover (drop-offs, logs, rocks, etc.) is nearby. So when you approach a lake look carefully for trout cruising in the shallows or holding near cover in the shallow water.

I've approached many alpine lakes where trout were rising in the deeper water tempting me to wade in or climb a rock and make the long cast first. Most of the time these turn out to be the lake's small trout and on too many occasions I've spooked big trout from the shallows in my haste to get at the risers.

So fish the shallows first. If the air is still and you can see into the water look carefully for trout and trout cover (good polarized sunglasses, incidentally, are mandatory for alpine-lake fishing).

If a breeze ripples the water so you can't see below the surface just assume the trout are there and fish shallow first. Alpine-lake trout often cruise shallow water along more-or-less regular routes, sometimes alone or sometimes in small, loosely organized packs.

If you can see a cruising trout and determine its speed and direction of travel it becomes pretty a easy mark. Cast a small nymph or wet fly well ahead of the fish and in line with its direction of travel and allow the fly to sink to the bottom or at least to the trout's level. When the fish approaches within two or three feet of the fly, give the nymph two or three quick, short twitches.

The "Littoral zone" of a lake is that area where light penetration is sufficient to allow plant growth. Along with plant growth comes a variety of aquatic organisms on which trout can feed.

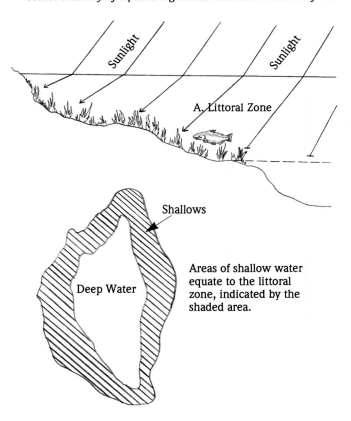

Assuming you have made a quiet, accurate cast and assuming the fish have maintained their course, one of two things will happen: If cruising alone a trout will often amble over and sip in the fly rather leisurely; if traveling in a small school the fish are basically competing with one another, so one or more may rush the fly with startling suddenness as soon as they see it move.

Sometimes you will encounter cruising trout that are spooky enough that they will not tolerate a fly or leader dimpling the surface ahead of them or anywhere within their visual range no matter how delicate the cast. I fish a lake in Oregon's Mt. Jefferson Wilderness where this is invariably the case on still mornings.

The rainbows in this lake run 16- to 18-inches during a good year and seem to have grown to those proportions by being exceptionally wary. Having spooked these fish by casting ahead of them as they cruised near shore I soon learned to employ a dif-

turn and I would have to find another. Other times the fish would pass by too far from its original path and my fly would escape unnoticed. But if the fly and the fish were within five feet of one another I would virtually always draw a strike.

I've experimented with these trout because that particular lake has always been ideal for sight fishing tactics. Sometimes I would wait until the trout was virtually on top of the fly and only then would I impart a slight twitch. The trout would practically turn a somersault to get at the fly.

On numerous occasions I tried both tiny nymphs and oversized nymphs. Both would work although a No. 4 Woolly Worm or Dragonfly Nymph would sometimes spook the fish when not allowed to settle all the way to the bottom.

A large nymph allowed to settle all the way to the bottom and then twitched sharply out of the mud, leaving a cloud of de-

Keeping low to the ground, DeAnn Montgomery casts to trout cruising around this inlet.

ferent tactic. First I would stand back from the shore and wait for a trout to cruise by in the shallows. When one appeared I would note its direction and its distance from shore. After the fish passed out of range I would flip a No. 10 Hare's Ear or Carey Special into the lake and allow it to settle to the bottom along the trout's previous route.

Then I would wait. On this particular lake I would often wait for four or five minutes because the trout patrolled rather large cruising circuits. Sometimes a second trout would appear nearby before the original trout returned. More often, I would wait the full four or five minutes before the original trout returned casually hunting side to side in search of food.

When the trout approached to within three or four feet of the spot where my fly had settled to the bottom I would give a sharp twitch, causing the fly to jump from the bottom. I would follow with two more short, quick strips but would rarely have time to make a third as the trout, his attention captured by the initial movement, would charge and grab the fly.

It didn't always work out. Sometimes the trout didn't re-

bris closely mimics the actions of a dragonfly nymph jetting from the bottom. The mud dwelling dragonflies common to the alpine lakes ambush their prey by burying themselves in the bottom debris. When ambushing prey or when escaping predators these nymphs forcefully expel a jet of water through their anal cavity that is capable of driving them through three to eight inches of water quite rapidly, usually trailing a cloud of debris. Trout learn to recognize this suddenly appearing debris cloud as a feeding opportunity and will readily investigate.

The behavior of these dragonfly nymphs is perfectly imitated by a weighted pattern being pulled suddenly from the bottom in a wash of debris. In a clear mountain lake, any trout within five or six feet (sometimes considerably more) will rush to grab the fly.

Once in a while, however, I have encountered trout that ignore a fly twitched from the bottom in front of them. These trout have, in virtually every case, lived in lakes with a fair amount of fishing pressure and even then only become suspicious during bright, still days. With my brother Mike, I fished a small lake in Washington's Alpine Lakes Wilderness where we could not interest cruising trout in chasing nymphs fished in the manner described above. Our solution, eventually, was to cast into the deeper water beyond a fairly steep drop-off, allow the fly to settle to the bottom out there and then crawl it along the bottom—ever so slowly—into the shallower water. We began hooking rainbows right along the drop off.

In any case sight-fishing tactics are always the most exciting ways to fish alpine lakes. Unfortunately, however, still water and good light (along with the mandatory pair of polarized glasses) are required for sight fishing. As often as not a breeze will ripple the surface of the high lakes.

Unsettled water means two things for fly anglers: Little opportunity for sight fishing on the one hand but less-spooky trout on the other. When wind, rain or both stir a lake's surface, trout emboldened by the cover of rippled water become more aggressive, less flighty and easier to approach.

The basic strategy of fishing shallows first still applies but now you will be fishing blind rather than casting to individual fish. Cover the water thoroughly by casting in a half clock fashion: first cast toward 9:00 then 10:00, 11, 12, 1, 2, and 3:00. Repeat the process a time or two then move to a new location and try again.

Tim Blount fishes a likely looking shoal/drop-off area of a high lake in Wyoming.

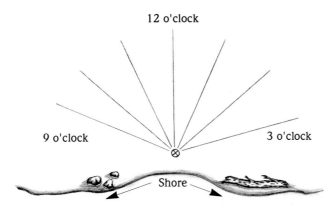

The "round-the-clock" casting strategy allows you to effectively cover the water when you cannot see below the surface.

Remember to pay special attention to all the structural elements found in the shallows. These include any inlets and outlets. Trout congregate around inlets to look for various food items being washed into the lake or to find cooler water; they hover near outlets at times because the pull of the water washes ants, mayfly spinners and countless other organisms toward them. Always cast a fly near submerged or floating timber and toward boulders no matter how barren the area might look. Trout can find a way to hide even in the sparsest of cover. I have also found trout hiding under overhanging willows or other shrubbery, especially where branches reach the water's surface.

Once you have covered the shallows (by sight fishing in calm water or by blind fishing in rippled water) start in on the deeper water, again focusing first on structural elements like submerged boulders, steep drop-offs, deep weedbeds and water-

logged timber. Often times a 10-foot sinktip line will help get a fly down quickly in deeper water. (Incidentally, I often choose a sink-tip line rather than a full sinker because the floating section remains on the water's surface when stripped in during the retrieve; sinking lines will sink down around your feet during the retrieve often getting caught on things, although they are a better choice on bright, still days because the entire line sinks below the surface, eliminating wakes and line shadows.)

In addition to the structural elements pay special attention to the windward and leeward sides of an alpine lake. The wind-

Casting from an old fallen tree, Dewey Weddington fishes the shoreline structure of this lake in Oregon's Waldo Lake Wilderness.

ward side is the side from which the wind is blowing; ne leeward side is the opposite side, toward which the wind blows. If the windward shoreline is cloaked in timber or shrubbery you can expect a stiff breeze to blow ants, beetles, spiders and other terrestrials into the lake below, offering an easy meal to the trout.

Similarly, a steady breeze from one direction will eventually congregate countless insects on the leeward shoreline attracting trout to that side of the lake. I once fished a small, funnel-shaped lake that was oriented lengthwise to a prevailing wind that had been blowing hard for four days. A tremendous *Callibaetis* mayfly hatch had been underway for the better part of a week and the leeward end of this lake soon became covered with a carpet of dead mayfly spinners. There must have been 200 insects in every square foot of a good acre of water.

At first the trout fed greedily on the spinners and were relatively easy to catch. But by the end of the week so many insects had blown to the end of the lake that hooking a trout on my imitation was a mere chance occurrence: If I could put the fly three or four feet in front of a cruising trout I figured I had about a one in 500 chance of having the fish choose my fly over all those naturals. Eventually I figured out that I could catch a few fish on a wet fly but the dry-fly fishing was entirely futile.

Assuming you fish around the log beforehand you can use large fallen trees as casting platforms.

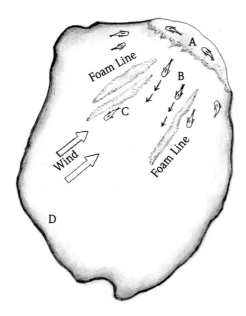

Trout in the high lakes respond to surface foods concentrated by winds. Any of several feeding strategies might be employed on the leeward side of the lake: A. Trout may cruise along the immediate shoreline where debris (including food) is concentrated. B. Fish may simply swim into the wind just below the surface sipping whatever insects they find. C. They may rise to insects trapped in any debris lines or foam lines that form on the surface. If trees or brush line the windward shore you can expect, during a heavy breeze, to find trout looking for terrestrials and other insects blown into the water from overhanging branches(D).

That was an extreme case (although I've seen the same thing occur several times) but it illustrates the point that alpine-lake anglers should always pay attention to what the wind is doing.

Incidentally, trout that are feeding on a large volume of wind-drifted insects can become rather selective, especially where *Callibaetis* mayflies (see Chapter 3) are involved. Most of this discussion to this point however, has been predicated by the assumption that you are fishing for nonselective trout which do not exhibit a specific feeding behavior but are instead searching for whatever morsels they can find.

In fact, alpine trout in most lakes have little choice but to feed non-selectively and at times ravenously for the few short months during which the lakes are free of ice. Because of this nonselective behavior amongst alpine trout, you might expect fairly easy fishing. Often enough, given a careful approach, alpine trout do indeed prove cooperative.

But every once in a while the insatiable appetite of these fish has a flip-side—a catch 22 of sorts—that rears its ugly head during the occasional periods of super-dense insect emergences or terrestrial drifts. At such times, high-altitude trout may feed so aggressively for short periods of time that they quite literally stuff themselves into inactivity.

Brent Snow of Eugene, Oregon tells a great story that illustrates this point perfectly. Brent had hiked into a lake high in the Eagle Cap Wilderness during one of those years when grasshopper populations had exploded even at high altitudes. The

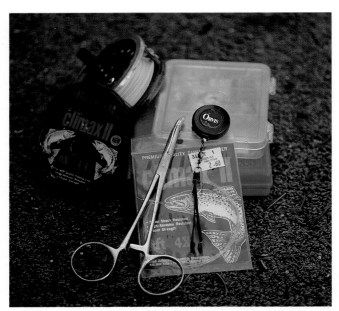

Tackle for alpine-lake fishing should be kept to a minimum when long backpacking trips are involved.

lake that Brent fished just happened to be situated in a place where prevailing winds deposited thousands of grasshoppers onto the water. Despite the potential for great fishing, Brent's timing was off: He arrived at the lake too late and the trout had been feeding on the hoppers for several days. The fish were gorged to the point that only an occasional foraging trout would take even a passing interest in any fly Brent cast.

Had Brent arrived a few days earlier he would have been telling fish-catching stories well into the night. But once in a while we play that roulette game with alpine trout: During times of prolific insect abundance trout can be tough to catch simply because they stuff themselves into inactivity. Hoppers, ants, beetles, *Callibaetis* mayflies, chironomids or even damsels can be the

All-purpose wet flies for alpine lakes. Top: Partridge & Orange, Timberline Emerger, Soft-hackle Zug Bug, Zug Bug Bottom: Pheasant Tail Nymph, Gold Ribbed Hare's Nymph.

culprit in times of high insect density.

On several lakes where I've encountered those super-heavy *Callibaetis* hatches, timing has proved to be everything. Arrive during the first few days of the emergence and fishing is superb. After that, however, the fish feed for shorter periods of time each day and sometimes seem more interested in kicking back in an easy chair, lighting a pipe and leisurely digesting a big meal.

Luckily these situations are not the norm. Many alpine lakes simply are not fertile enough to support huge densities of any given trout food nor geographically situated to intercept many heavy terrestrial flights. In addition, selective feeding opportunities for

Ideal trout water on this Montana lake: A steep leeward shoreline with fallen timber, shoreline brush and food items concentrated by the wind.

most alpine-lake trout occupy only short periods of the summer on the more fertile lakes. In many high lakes trout never feed selectively simply because they never have occasion to do so; in other lakes trout get picky only once in a great while.

Therefore, given a well-executed and stealthy approach, fly anglers can usually expect reasonably uncomplicated fishing on the high lakes—our justified reward for long hikes. Most of the time basic attractor-type patterns catch trout. Some of the best include various Soft Hackles (like the Partridge and Orange), Zug Bugs, small Woolly Buggers and Hare's Ear Nymphs. These, of course, are all wet flies designed to be fished sub surface where most of the feeding activity occurs in the high lakes.

Except during mayfly, midge and caddis hatches, most surface-feeding trout are simply taking what they can find—an ant here, a beetle there; a spent mayfly or a dead moth. Thus when you have the opportunity to cast to cruising trout that are feeding on top, virtually any dry fly will work. I've had especially good success with ant patterns, Gulpher Specials, Griffith's Gnats and renegades. You could just as well add dozens of other patterns

General Purpose Flies For Alpine Lakes

Gold Ribbed Hare's Ear Nymph

Hook: Wet fly, 2XL, No. 8-14 (Partridge #SH1)

Tail: Brown partridge fibers

Body: Natural hare's mask fur

Rib: Fine or small gold oval

Thorax: Natural dark hare's mask fur

Shellback: Turkey tail section

Elk Hair Caddis (Al Troth)

Hook: Dry fly, No. 10-14 (Partridge #L4A)

Body: Fur dubbing, olive, brown or tan

Rib: Fine wire or monofilament

Hackle: Brown or dun, palmered

Wing: Elk hair

Gulper Special (Al Troth)

Hook: Dry fly, No. 12-18 (Partridge #L4A)

Tail: Grizzly hackle fibers

Body: Olive dubbing or dun dubbing

Wing: Gray poly yarn tied in as post

Hackle: Grizzly or dun (or both) tied parachute style

Partridge & Orange (Sylvester Nemes)

Hook: Wet fly, No. 10-14 (Partridge #G3A)

Body: Orange silk

Thorax: Two turns of natural hare's mask fur

Hackle: Natural brown or gray partridge

Kaufmann Timberline Emerger (Randall Kaufmann)

Hook: Wet fly, No. 10-16 (Partridge #G3A)

Tail: Short moose hairs or pheasant tail fibers

Body: Gray dubbing

Hackle: Brown

Wings: Grizzly hackle tips, tied back in style of wet fly

Soft Hackle Zug Bug

Hook: Wet fly, 2XL, No. 8-12 (Partridge #SH1)

Tail: Peacock sword

Body: Peacock herl

Rib: Fine silver or gold oval, counter-wrapped

Hackle: Two to three turns of partridge or olive-dyed partridge

Zug Bug

Hook: Wet fly, 2XL, No. 8-14 (Partridge #SH1)

Tail: Peacock sword

Body: Peacock herl

Rib: Fine silver or gold oval, counter-wrapped

Wingpad: Lemon woodduck

Throat: Brown hackle fibers

Flying Fur Ant

Hook: Dry fly, No. 12-16 (Partridge #L4A)

Body: Two distinct segments of black fur

Hackle: Two to three turns of black hackle between body segments

Wings: Dun or grizzly hackle tips, tied delta style or dun Z-Lon tied spent

Pheasant Tail Nymph

Hook: Wet fly, 2XL, No. 8-14 (Partridge #SH1)

Tail: Pheasant tail fibers

Body: Pheasant tail fibers

Rib: Fine copper wire (counter)

Thorax: Peacock herl

Shellback: Pheasant tail fibers

Legs: Pheasant tail fibers

Woolly Bugger

Hook: 3XL nymph, No. 6-10 (Partridge #SH3)

Tail: Marabou and a few strands of Flashabou

Body: Chenille

Hackle: saddle, palmered

Rib: Fine wire, counterwrapped

Colors: All black; olive; green body/black tail; olive-brown body/brown tail

---

to that list and be certain of hooking nonselective surface feeders.

One of the best tactics for these nonselective surface feeding trout is to impart an occasional gentle twitch in the fly as it sits on the water. This twitch might mimic a struggling insect unwittingly trapped on the water or just might catch the trout's attention. Whatever the case, the tactic often works wonders whether you are casting to visible fish or are simply covering the water.

Tackle for Alpine Lakes

Long hikes into remote lakes require that you consider the weight and bulk of your fly tackle along with your other gear. This includes fly boxes. I carry two medium-sized boxes, one with wet flies, streamers and nymphs; the other with dry flies. For nymphs, wet flies and streamers I prefer the plastic boxes with foam ridges for the flies. For dry flies I use a plastic compartmentalized box to avoid crushing hackles. These boxes float should you accidentally drop one in the lake and they are lighter in weight than similar metal boxes.

Organize your boxes according to the duration of your trip (i.e. longer trip, more flies) and according to the type of fishing you expect to encounter. If you can fit all your flies into one box by all means do so. Choose your tackle items wisely: leader nippers, tippet material, extra leaders, small needle-nose pliers, a small flashlight, fly floatant, strike indicators, floating and sinking (and/or sink tip) lines.

An eight- to nine-foot rod capable of handling a four-, five- or six-weight line is ideal for alpine lakes. The four-piece models that fit into short tubes are great for backpacking.

General Purpose Patterns for Alpine Lakes:

The list of patterns represents my favorite general searching type flies for alpine lakes. In addition to those listed above some of the patterns listed for specific trout foods in Chapter 3 make very good searching patterns. These include the damsel nymphs, Alpine Dragon Fly Nymph, scud patterns and water beetle patterns, Peeking Caddis, Griffith's Gnat and chironomid pupa.

Fishing The Hatch: Selective High-Lake Trout

At times alpine-lake anglers must still deal with good old-fashioned selectivity just as if fishing a hatch on a good trout stream. The *Callibaetis* mayfly (speckled-wing dun) emergence, even when sparse, often triggers selective feeding, as does a decent chironomid (midge) emergence. Damsel nymphs as well as adults on occasion can cause selective feeding behavior on lakes with heavy weed growth. These three insects—speckled-wing duns, midges and damsels—are responsible for the vast majority of selective feeding on alpine lakes.

Once in a while, however, you will encounter selective feeding on water beetles, scuds (freshwater shrimp), dragonfly nymphs, caddis, snails or leeches. When alpine lake trout react selectively to these aquatic organisms they generally do so only in lakes (or parts of lakes) where the prey in question is abundant for brief periods. Dragonfly nymphs, for example, are found in all the high lakes, but rarely in sufficient numbers to trigger selective feeding. Still, while dragonflies emerge sporadically in most lakes, some of the more fertile waters host concentrated hatches that can trigger selective feeding by trout. Similar scenarios occur at times with caddisflies.

In any event, while fishing alpine lakes you can expect to encounter selective feeding on *Callibaetis* mayflies and midges; sometimes on damsels. Selective feeding on other organisms is much less common on alpine lakes.

Still you should be prepared to deal with selective trout when you encounter them: Fairly precise imitation is the solution. In other words, match the hatch.

On a high lake in Oregon Tim Blount employs the "cast–wait–skate"
routine wherein he casts a dry caddis pattern, waits several minutes and then skates the
fly a foot or two before waiting again. This tactic can prove highly effective not to mention rather exciting.

A swarm of recently emerged adult damsels cluster on a partially submerged branch.

Callibaetis Mayfly (Speckled-Wing Dun)

The *Callibaetis* is by far the most common mayfly (and generally the only one of consequence) on alpine lakes. The mayfly emergence begins anytime between mid-June and late July depending on location and elevation and can last until the snow falls in some areas. The peak emergence usually occurs between late July and mid-September. Ranging from grayish-tan to light ashy gray to pale olive-tan in color, these mayflies have characteristic mottled bodies and wings.

These insects can vary in size but seem to get smaller as the season progresses. A No. 14 imitation may mimic the early hatches perfectly, while 16s or 18s will be required later during the summer and early fall. I've never found specific body color to matter to alpine trout during a *Callibaetis* emergence but the fish can be selective to size, especially during a heavy hatch. Also, trout will at times key on *Callibaetis* nymphs as they swim to the surface. In such cases the fish can't resist a sparse Hare's Ear Nymph, Shewey *Callibaetis* nymph or similar pattern.

Trout feeding on *Callibaetis* emergers frequently divulge their preference by disturbing the water's surface with their tails or dorsal fins or sometimes just with a slight swirl or "bulge." Splashy rises or "gulping" rises (usually leaving air bubbles behind) on the other hand, indicate surface feeding.

In addition, trout tend to feed actively near the bottom prior to *Callibaetis* hatches because the mayfly nymphs get restless about an hour before they actually begin to hatch. If you are familiar with the timing of the hatch on a particular lake you can begin fishing nymphs with short, darting movements one to two hours prior to emergence. If you're not sure when the hatch will begin just watch for the first few duns that often emerge well before the main hatch.

When the emergence does begin in earnest and trout are rising everywhere for duns, you need only cast your mayfly imitation toward a group of feeding fish and wait. Often a few gentle twitches of the fly after it has remained motionless for 15 to 30 seconds will help draw a strike.

Frequently during the *Callibaetis* hatch you can cast ahead

Callibaetis *(speckled-wing dun) mayfly patterns: top to bottom: Shewey* Callibaetis *Nymph,* Callibaetis *Soft Hackle,* Callibaetis *Gulper Special, Parachute Adams,* Callibaetis *Krystal Spinner,* Callibaetis *Compara-dun.*

Callibaetis Mayfly Patterns

Parachute Adams
Hook: Dry fly, No. 14-18 (Partridge #L3A or L4A)
Tail: Grizzly and brown hackle fibers
Body: Light gray dubbing
Wing: White poly yarn or calf body hair
Hackle: Grizzly-brown mixed, parachute style

Shewey *Callibaetis* Nymph
Hook: Nymph, No. 12-16 (Partridge #K12ST)
Tail: Three pheasant tail fibers
Body: Brown dubbing
Rib: Fine gold wire
Thorax: Olive-brown ostrich herl
Shellback: Bronze turkey tail or copper Krystal Flash
Legs: Pheasant tail fibers

Callibaetis Gulper Special
Hook: Dry fly, No. 14-18 (Partridge #L3A or L4A)
Tail: Grizzly hackle fibers
Body: Light tan dubbing
Wing: Poly yarn, white or gray
Hackle: Grizzly, 3 to 5 turns parachute style

Callibaetis Comparadun
Hook: Dry fly, No. 14-18 (Partridge #L3A or L4A)
Tail: Hackle fibers or Micro-fibets, divided
Body: Light tan dubbing
Wing: Fine natural deer hair, flared to form upright wing

Callibaetis Soft-Hackle
Hook: Wet fly, No. 12-16 (Partridge #L2A)
Tail: Short gray partridge fibers
Body: Tan dubbing
Collar: Brown partridge or grouse, sparse

Callibaetis Krystal Spinner
Hook: Dry fly, No. 14-18 (Partridge #L3A or L4A)
Tails: Micro-fibets, divided
Body: Pale whitish-tan dubbing
Wings: Four to six strands of pearl Krystal Flash, spent
Hackle: Watery dun and grizzly mixed, wrapped below, behind and in front of wings (and over the top of dubbing), then clipped flush

Pheasant Tail Nymph
Hook: Nymph, No. 12-16 (Partridge #SH2)
Tail: 3-5 pheasant tail fibers
Body: Pheasant tail fibers
Rib: Fine gold or copper wire
Thorax: Peacock herl
Shellback: Pheasant tail fibers
Legs: Brown partridge fiber

of a particular fish and intercept it. Just watch for a good fish steadily swimming along and gulping a mayfly every couple feet. The larger trout in a lake often feed in this manner (which is called gulping because of the sound made by the fish when they rise for a bug) while the smaller fish splash noisily with no apparent strategy in mind.

During a fairly heavy emergence a gulper will rise methodically while cruising leisurely in a particular direction. Watch two or three rises in a row so you can determine the space between them. Having figured out this "rise interval," cast far enough ahead so that your fly stands a good chance of being in the right place at the right time. In other words, if the trout rises every two feet cast your fly four to six feet ahead of the last riseform and in line with the last several. Then wait.

All too often a trout will change direction on you, sometimes just enough to miss your fly by inches. Then the fish will rise to a natural just inches from your fly as if to spite you. Pick up as soon as the fish passes and cast ahead of it again. I found a particularly troublesome rainbow on a lake in Oregon's Mt. Jefferson Wilderness: During a heavy *Callibaetis* hatch this fish took 14 casts before finally taking my fly. Each time I thought I had it right only to have the fish take a real bug just inches from the fly. After seven or eight tries the fish slowly turned around and gave me another shot not unlike a tin duck in a state-fair shooting gallery.

As for the emerger patterns try a floating line and a long leader. Allow the fly to sink a few inches, perhaps as far as a foot or so, then retrieve with short strips, quickly at first but slow when the fly reaches the surface. Trout take emerger and nymph patterns as they sink, so keep an eye on the leader coils or the end of the fly line for any sudden movement.

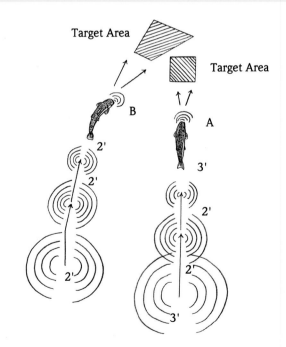

Gulping trout: When feeding on the surface during a heavy hatch some trout will simply swim along and rise at more or less regular intervals. In example A, the trout is swimming a straight line and rising every two or three feet. You must cast to an area perhaps two rise intervals ahead of the trout (i.e. 4-6 feet) and allow the fly to sit still until the trout either takes it or passes by. In example B, the trout is swimming in an arc-shaped route. Not only must you estimate the rise interval but you must also guess at the trout's exact direction of travel.

You can cast nymphs and soft hackles to individual fish if they are visible but *Callibaetis* hatches often occur in the afternoon when light mountain breezes ripple the water. Therefore, if you can't see individual fish, cast to areas of concentrated surface activity or make searching casts in the two- to eight-foot depths where the mayflies usually occur.

Callibaetis spinner falls often draw the attention of trout as well. These spinner flights can invade the shoreline shallows any time of day but are most common from noon through early evening. Since the spinners gather over shallow water, usually near shore, trout can be especially spooky. The same Parachute Adams or Gulper Special used to imitate the dun will fool most spinner-feeding trout. Sometimes more selective fish may demand that you switch to a spinner pattern such as the *Callibaetis* Krystal Spinner.

Chironomids (midges)

Like the *Callibaetis* mayflies, chironomids (midges) can sometimes emerge in dense enough numbers to trigger selective feeding amongst alpine-lake trout. In form chironomids look like mosquitos (to which they are closely related). Their color can vary considerably but is rarely important to alpine trout. Size, however, can be critical. Some species of alpine-lake midges can be imitated with No. 12, 14 and 16 flies; others, unfortunately, require hooks in the No. 18-24 category.

Chironomid (midge) patterns—Top:
Adult Midge and Harrop CDC Emerging Midge
Middle: Shewey's Revertical Midge Emerger Lower: Shewey's
Deep-water Midge Pupa and Kimball's Diptera Emerger.

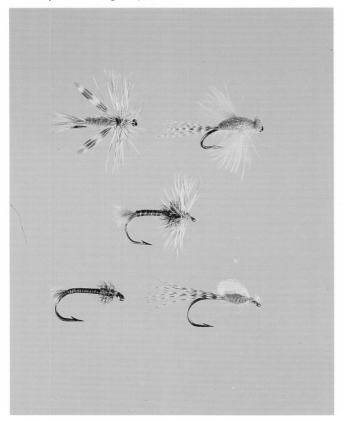

Large cutthroat from small lake in Idaho's
Sawtooth Wilderness.

Chironomids are the most abundant aquatic trout foods in the alpine lakes, sometimes reaching unbelievable densities. At times, in fact, midges comprise the bulk of the trout's diet in many alpine waters. On alpine lakes midges can hatch at several times with mid-day and late evening emergences being common. On some lakes, chironomids seem to hatch virtually all day. These hatches occur all over the lake from the deepest parts in the middle to the shallowest shoreline margins. In this way, the chironomid hatches differ markedly from emergences of mayflies and caddis which do not thrive in or hatch from areas of deep water. So, if you see fish rising steadily in an area of very deep water you can safely assume midges are the culprit (unless wind or currents are carrying other insects out there).

Most often, the emerging pupa of these insects comprise the bulk of a fish's take, although adults, when they remain on the water for any length of time, are taken as well. These chironomid pupa hang in the surface film during the actual emergence making high-floating imitations largely ineffective when trout feed selectively. I usually opt for a three-fly setup when fish get picky with midges: The lead fly and the first dropper, spaced 18 inches apart, are pupa imitations designed to either sink a few inches or hang in the surface film. Eighteen inches above the second dropper I attach a Griffith's Gnat, which is a dry pattern meant to imitate an adult midge or a cluster of adults (they often cling together after emerging, especially in cold weather). More importantly, this dry fly serves as a strike indicator for the sunken flies. Even the most subtle take will cause this indicator fly to twitch on the surface.

Obviously this system requires a long leader with a five- or six-foot tippet. Cast to a cluster of rises and let the lead flies sink. For the first minute or so, sweat it out and resist the temptation to move the flies. Then begin a retrieve comprised of short strips interspersed with 10 second pauses. If a trout picks up one of the pupa patterns during the pause you will see a sudden twitch (sometimes just a slight inching) of the indicator fly. Gently raise the rod tip. Should you have a chance to cast to gulping trout, lead them by a couple of rise intervals so the pupa imitation has time to penetrate the surface film and sink an inch or two.

A beautifully marked brook trout from Wyoming.

Windy evenings in the high country often wreck havoc on chironomids: First, a choppy surface makes the pupa's emergence through the film more difficult. Therefore, tremendous numbers of pupa can at times become more or less trapped at and just below the surface creating easy pickings for trout. Second, adult midges can be blown en masse onto the surface where they are consequently stranded, unable to escape. These dead and dying midges will drift with the wind eventually being concentrated along leeward shorelines. Both of these occurrences create good dry line opportunity for anglers.

In addition, pupa patterns fished near the bottom can effectively imitate that stage of the chironomid's life where the insect leaves the cover of the mud and sediments in order to ascend to the surface. Again I prefer a two- or three-fly setup using the deep water midge pupa pattern. If I'm not sure of the insect's actual color, this dropper system allows me to try two or three colors simultaneously until I determine whether trout have a preference. On alpine lakes, the fish rarely care much about color so long as the chironomid pupa imitation looks edible.

In reasonably deep water, say 10 feet or more, I employ a full sinking line for fishing midge pupa near the bottom. A slow, short retrieve pattern interspersed with pauses seems to be the most effective method of fishing pupa near the bottom. In water less than ten feet deep a floating line coupled with a long, light leader enables you to fish midge pupa along the bottom and also allows for a lifting retrieve whereby you slowly swim the pupa toward the surface: After the pupa has sunk to the bottom with the leader suspended somewhat vertically, begin a retrieve of several slow, short strips followed by a pause of about five seconds. Repeat this pattern until the fly reaches the surface.

As you retrieve the fly in this manner keep the first few

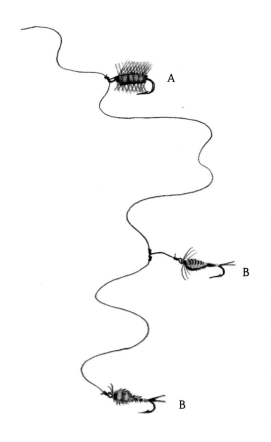

Leaders set-up for chironomid fishing:
A. Griffith's Gnat as first dropper (doubles as the strike indicator). B. Pupa pattern as second dropper and as lead fly.

Chironomid Patterns

CDC Emerging Midge
(Rene' Harrop)
Hook: Fine wire dry fly, No. 16-22 (Partridge #L4A)
Tail: Teal flank
Shellback: Gray Evazote foam material
Body: Poly dubbing to match natural
Head: Gray Evazote (continuation of shellback)

Shewey's Deep-water Midge Pupa
Hook: Wet fly, No. 14-22 (Partrdige #G3A)
Tail: Minute tuft of gray ostrich fiber
Body: Stripped peacock herl (bleached and colored with waterproof marker to arrive at appropriate shade)
Rib: Fine copper wire (omit on tiniest sizes)
Head/thorax: A few turns of herl from eye of peacock tail quill (use the bronze-colored herl)

Kimball's Diptera Emerger
(Mike Kimball)
Hook: Fine wire dry fly, No. 16-26 (Partridge #L4A)
Tail: teal flank, tied long and splayed to represent pupa's trailing shuck
Thorax: Dubbed fur or poly, color to match natural
Legs: Gray CDC feather
Wingcase: Small strand of white or light gray poly yarn, tied in to form exaggerated hump at the rear of the case and a gradual slope toward the eye of the hook

Griffith's Gnat (George Griffith)
Hook: Dry fly, No. 14-20 (Partridge #L4A)
Body: Fine peacock herl
Hackle: Grizzly, palmered through body
Rib: Fine wire or tying thread

Re-Vertical Midge Emerger
Hook: Fine wire dry fly, No. 14-22 (Partridge #L4A)
Tail: Minute puff of white feather fluff
Body: fine peacock herl, stripped until last two to four turns
Rib: Fine gold wire (omit on tiniest sizes)
Hackle: Very stiff dry fly hackle tied against the eye of the hook; 2-4 turns

Adult Chironomid
Hook: Dry fly, No. 14-24 (Partridge #L4A)
Tails: A few grizzly hackle fibers, short and fanned
Body: Dubbed fur, to match color of natural or a simple pale gray or cream
Wings: Grizzly hackle tips, delta-style
Hackle: A few turns of grizzly in front of wings; clipped below

---

inches of the rod tip just below the surface so you can feel even the most delicate of strikes.

Chironomid larvae, despite being abundant in most lakes, are not nearly as significant to trout as the pupa. Most midge larvae live within the bottom sediment and are thus largely unavailable to fish. But the pupa as they rise to the surface during emergence and as they struggle to escape their pupal shucks (a process that can take quite some time in many cases) are entirely vulnerable.

Dry damsel patterns: Left: Shewey's Emergent Damsel Cripple. Right: Adult Blue Damsel.

Damselflies

Chironomids, along with the aforementioned *Callibaetis* mayflies, are responsible for the majority of selective feeding on high lakes when it does occur. Once in a while you find an exceptionally weedy lake where trout key in on damsel nymphs during the mid-morning hours of July or early August days.

Between 8 a.m. and noon (8 to 10 a.m. on warm mornings, noonish on cold mornings) the damsel nymphs begin their shoreward migration, where they seek reeds, grass, logs, rocks, even you or your float tube or any object on which they can crawl from the water. These nymphs swim with a vigorous side-to-side wiggling motion, appearing to expend a great deal of energy per amount of forward progress.

Such nymph activity gets trout excited and after a few days of heavy damsel emergences the trout seem to anticipate the beginning of the migration each morning. I've seen fish literally lined up in shallow water waiting for the nymphs to start their perilous swim toward shore: On a gem of a lake in Wyoming's Fitzpatrick Wilderness I stumbled onto an army of small brook trout literally lining one shoreline in what appeared to be a rather orderly rank and file. The sparse, short weeds growing along the bottom near the shore proved to be a haven for an impressive number of olive damsel nymphs, which soon began leaving the protective green cover and wiggling slowly toward the grass. At that point the trout simply broke ranks and went berserk. Watching this proved more entertaining than fishing, especially since the brookies all ran about five inches in length.

A simple Marabou Damsel Nymph pattern fished so that you can retrieve toward shore or other objects protruding from the water will prove highly productive. Damsel nymphs live in the

Damsel Patterns

Shewey's Woodduck Damsel Nymph

Hook: 2X-long nymph hook, No. 10-12 (Partridge # K12ST or SH4)

Tail: A few strands of wide marabou fluff

Body: Marabou fibers tied in by the tips and wrapped up the hook shank and topped with a mixture of lemon wood duck fibers and olive Krystal Flash

Rib: Fine gold wire, counterwrapped

Thorax: Marabou, wrapped on shank

Legs: Olive-dyed partridge, tied in by tip and pulled over thorax

Shellback: Lemon woodduck feather tied in behind thorax and pulled forward over top of partridge feather

Colors: Light, bright olive; medium olive, tan

Shewey's Damp Damsel Nymph

Hook: Wet fly, No. 12 (Partridge #SH4)

Tail: Marabou fluff

Body: Marabou fibers wrapped up hook shankrib: fine gold wire, counter-wrapped

Thorax: Marabou wrapped over shank

Legs: olive-dyed partridge palmered through thorax (Three turns; one side of feather stripped away)

Shellback: Closed cell foam strip

Emergent Damsel Cripple

Hook: Dry fly, No. 12 (Partridge #L3A or L4A)

Body: Pale olive bucktail, extended

Wing: Tan Z-Lon, spent

Hackle: Two to three turns of light dun

Adult Blue Damsel

Hook: Dry fly, No. 12 (Partridge #L3A or L4A)

Thread: Black 6/0

Body: Blue bucktail, extended

Post: Butt ends of bucktail used for body

Wings: Five to six strands of pearl Krystal Flash

Hackle: Two to three turns of dun or grizzly, parachute-style

Marabou Damsel Nymph

Hook: 2XL or 3XL nymph, No. 10-14 (Partridge #SH4)

Tail: Marabou

Body: Marabou wrapped on shank

Rib: Fine gold wire

Thorax/Legs: Tuft of marabou tied in the wing position

---

aquatic weeds, so concentrate your efforts over the areas of dense vegetation. Shades of olive, green and tan are common nymph colors but alpine trout are usually forgiving in terms of precise shade.

Sometimes trout feed on the newly emerged adults, usually when a stiff breeze accompanies the hatch blowing the bugs into the water before they can dry their wings for flying. The freshly hatched adults are usually a light olive color but will turn bright blue (males) or grayish-blue (females) upon maturity. Certain other species of damsel, which I have not encountered with regularity, may be dark green, brown or other colors upon maturity.

Some of the most exciting fishing of the season is possible when trout, especially big trout, will readily eat adult damsels. The rise is often explosive, sometimes throwing water for several feet in every direction. Other times the rise to adult damsels can be subtle leading you to think small fish. Then you set the hook into a trout larger than anything you expected from that lake. In any case, always carry a few imitations for adult damsels.

These adults frequently fly and hover just over the water's surface feeding greedily on chironomids and other small insects. In addition, the damsels often mate in flight over the water with both partners connected and trying to fly around together. Awkwardness prevails at times and the pair of damsels commonly end up in the water, especially when a breeze is present. Thus whether hunting or mating, adult damsels can and do become trout food. In fact, several times I've watched trout leap for hovering damsels.

Typically, these adult damsels trigger opportunistic feeding rather than selective feeding on the trout's part, but the nymphs and freshly-emerged adults can surely cause trout to feed selectively. At times I've found alpine trout rising explosively during the damsel emergence only to discover that their prey was damsel nymphs swimming or hanging right in the surface film. As a result I started tying and carrying floating damsel nymphs (I call the pattern a "damp damsel") designed to hang in the surface film.

Caddisflies

On many alpine lakes caddisflies represent an important part of the trout's diet. The cased larvae are taken readily and when the caddis hatches occur the pupa and adults can trigger selective feeding.

The most significant of the alpine lake caddis belong to the family Limnephilidae. These are case-making caddis and their shells are generally constructed of plant debris such as tiny twigs, parts of evergreen needles, parts of leaves, etc. In some instances the cases are constructed of fine sand or gravel.

These cased Limnephilid larvae crawl about on the bottom, often living amongst whatever scant vegetation exists or amongst decaying bottom debris. Alpine trout eat them case and all, although typically in an opportunistic rather than selective mode. The pupa and adults, however, are a different story: Both can be heavily preyed upon during morning, evening and night-time emergences.

These caddis pupa, which are often quite large, ascend steadily to the surface at emergence time and are thus entirely vulnerable to trout. The combination of a long leader, floating line and weighted pupa pattern allows you to sink the fly all the way to the bottom and then swim the imitation back to the surface by raising the rod tip smoothly and steadily. Since these caddis emergences occur in depths less than 10 or 12 feet this technique is fairly easy to use, especially from a float tube or when casting from shoreline rocks or other such natural casting platforms.

Sometimes you must cast over shallow water to place your fly within range of trout feeding on pupa. In these cases where you must extend the cast beyond 40 feet or so, making the imitation swim vertically to the surface will prove difficult without the aid of a sliding float on the leader.

I use a medium-sized "Corkie" (a hard foam float with a hole through the center often employed as a strike indicator) which I slide onto the leader. The Corkie remains on top while allowing the tippet and leader to slide through (you must use a well-weighted fly). As you retrieve the pupa pattern from the bottom, the Corkie guides the leader and tippet along a reasonable vertical path toward the surface.

This system has a couple drawbacks: First, you must use a long leader and tippet (I generally go with a nine-foot factory tapered leader and then add six more feet of tippet). This long leader when combined with the fly and Corkie becomes somewhat troublesome to cast. Second, the fly sometimes gets stuck in the Corkie during the cast and remains there when the whole works lands on the water with a resounding "splat." Should this problem occur simply tie a small loop in the tippet about 18 inches above the fly. This loop will act as a stopper not allowing the fly and Corkie to come in contact.

Despite these inherent potential difficulties, this Corkie method of fishing pupa allows you to enact a vertical retrieve on a long cast. For me the technique has proven valuable and highly effective on many occasions and I will sometimes employ two flies on the leader.

Upon emergence at the surface, adult Limnephilids frequently take a few moments to dry their wings before they fly away. Meanwhile, they often skitter about the surface attempting to take to the air. Naturally, these skating and skittering adults prove irresistible to trout. Fish will dash from several feet under water to take a shot at a caddis on the surface.

These adults are easily and effectively imitated with a dry pattern that is twitched and skated on the surface. Grease the fly and tippet with fly floatant and then deliver the cast toward rising trout. Allow the fly to sit still for a few seconds and then begin retrieving with erratic strips of line causing the caddis imitation to trail a gentle wake.

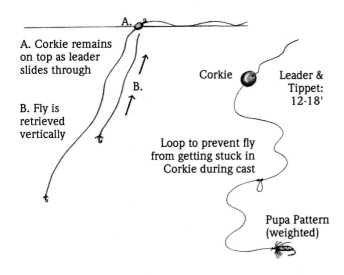

A. Corkie remains on top as leader slides through

B. Fly is retrieved vertically

Corkie

Leader & Tippet: 12-18'

Loop to prevent fly from getting stuck in Corkie during cast

Pupa Pattern (weighted)

Sliding Corkie set-up for fishing rising caddis pupa on a long line.

A cutthroat trout searches for food in the shallows with the cover of deep water just a flick of the tail away.

Incidentally, this tactic comes in handy at times when sparse, sporadic caddis hatches occur: I found a little lake in Montana's Lee Metcalf Wilderness that appeared fishless at first. After a while I noticed two large caddis skittering about on the surface trying to take flight. I watched them for several minutes and was just about convinced the lake held no fish when one of the insects disappeared in a violent splash. Seconds later the other caddis met its fate the same way.

I tied on a Soft Hackle Zug Bug and began casting allowing the fly to sink and then retrieving back. I reasoned that the trout must be feeding opportunistically with so few caddis on the water. However, more caddis appeared on the surface, always just one or two at a time. They would skitter about and occasionally fly away but just as often would be devoured by a trout. With each successive cast I lost more and more confidence in my wet fly. I knew the lake didn't hold many trout but those present seemed intent on eating what few caddis adults they could find.

Digging out my dry flies, I selected a No. 8 Jughead Caddis. I cast the fly across a small cove and waited for the splashdown rings to disappear. Then I began skating the fly back with slow, foot-long pulls of line. The third cast drew a strike and I beached a 12-inch cutthroat. That sporadic caddis emergence continued for another hour and I caught four trout by skating that Jughead on the surface.

Caddis and Alderfly Patterns

Black Alder Fly, Wet
Hook: Wet fly, No. 10-14 (Partridge #G3A)
Body: Peacock herl or black dubbing
Hackle: Two turns of starling hackle
Wing: Dark gray duck quill sections, tied wet fly style

Bucktail Caddis
Hook: Dry fly, 2XL, No. 6-14 or sedge No. 8-18 (Partridge #K12ST)
Body: Dubbed fur or wool, olive or tan
Hackle: brown, palmered
Wing: Natural brown deer hair dubbing

Black Alder Fly
Hook: Dry fly, No. 10-14 (Partridge #L3A)
Body: Black dubbing
Hackle: Black, palmered
Wing: Black deer hair

Elk Hair Caddis (Al Troth)
Hook: Dry fly, No. 10-14 (Partridge #L3A)
Body: Dubbing, olive, brown or tan
Rib: Fine gold wire
Hackle: Brown or grizzly, reverse palmered
Wing: Elk hair

Jughead Caddis
Hook: 2XL dry fly, No. 6-12 (Partridge #E1A)
Tail: Stacked deer hair, short (an aid to flotation)
Body: wool, olive or tan
Hackle: Brown, clipped short and palmered
Wing: deer hair
Head: Spun deer hair, clipped to form rather robust head

Peeking Caddis (George Anderson)
Hook: Wet fly, 2XL, No. 6-14 (Partridge #SH2 or H1A)
Body: Natural dark hare's mask fur
Rib: Fine gold oval (Optional)
Thorax: Two to three turns of olive or light tan
Legs: Partridge fibers
Head: Black ostrich

Alpine Caddis Pupa
Hook: Wet fly, No. 6-12 or sedge No. 8-18 (Partridge #K12ST)
Body: Fine dubbing spun in silk, olive or tan
Wingpads: Two small partridge feather tips
Antennae: Two long partridge fibers, trailing over back of fly
Throat: Partridge fibers
Head: Black ostrich

Similarly, Tim Blount and I discovered 16-inch brook trout in a tiny lake in Oregon's Three Sisters Wilderness Area. Casting and retrieving wet flies produced two trout but the commotion of casting again and again and fighting those two brookies prompted the rest of the fish to avoid our end of the lake like the plague. Tim tied on a No. 10 Caddis, cast as far out into the lake as he could, sat down on a log and waited. Every 10 or 15 seconds he would skate the fly 10 or 12 inches. The rises were nothing short of violent and Tim hooked three more brookies this way.

In any case, alpine lake caddis hatches, even sparse ones, can trigger selective feeding. Sometimes trout concentrate on the pupa below the surface, so if you encounter a substantial caddis emergence and don't see much surface activity accompanying the hatch, think pupa first.

Female caddis return to the lake during the afternoon or evening to lay eggs. In many cases this is accomplished when the insect drops to the water and skitters about feverishly, depositing the eggs just below the surface film. The sight of large caddisflies skittering about in this fashion will, of course, attract the attention of any nearby trout.

In addition to the caddisflies, some high lakes—most notably in the Cascade Range—provide habitat for black alderflies. These insects look like a caddis but the black or smoke-colored wings lack any evidence of tiny hairs like those found on the wings of caddisflies. Only the adults are of importance. High in the Cascades I have found lakes where at times black adlerflies swarm around the shoreline during the afternoon and frequently end up in the water. There they are greedily eaten by trout either on surface or under water (the adults often sink when they hit the water). On some occasions I have found trout hanging below swarming alderflies waiting for one to make a mistake. In this manner trout can act somewhat selective although having

had the opportunity to experiment rather extensively with alderflies on two lakes in particular, I have almost always been able to take these fish on virtually any smallish dry fly.

The first reference I ever found that discussed the alderflies I was fishing over on those lakes in the Oregon Cascades was *The Complete Book of Western Hatches,* by Rick Hafele and Dave Hughes. Watching alderflies struggle briefly on the surface and then disappear had led me to believe they were diving to lay eggs as some caddis do. But Hafele and Hughes note that this is inaccurate: Alderflies which actually lay their eggs on overhanging leaves and grasses, just plain sink when they hit the water. Because of this, Hafele and Hughes say that "the most successful imitation is dressed and fished as a wet fly."

Dragonflies

Dragonflies rarely cause trout to feed selectively on the alpine lakes, the exception being those times when on fertile waters dragonfly nymphs leave the protective cover of weedbeds en masse to seek rocks, logs and grass where they crawl from the water to emerge into winged adults.

This dragonfly emergence generally occurs between June and late July depending on elevation. Nymph imitations should be fished on the bottom near weedbeds or near areas of concentrated emergence with a slow, crawling retrieve interrupted occasionally with short, darting strips. These weed-dwelling dragonflies generally match their background color in shade with olives and greens being prevalent.

More important to the true alpine lakes are the mud-dwelling dragonfly nymphs which exhibit a shorter, more squat appearance than their weed-dwelling cousins. These mud-dwellers, as the name implies, live amongst the bottom debris of the high lakes where they wait in ambush for smaller aquatic

Shewey's Alpine Dragonfly Nymph

Hook: Streamer, 4XL, No. 6-10 (Partridge #D4A)

Abdomen: Seal fur or angora, dubbed over an underbody of chenille to form a football shape

Legs: Brown partridge hackle wrapped through a thin thorax of seal fur

Head: Seal fur or angora

Eyes: Monofilament eyes, colored black or dark brown

Shellback: Partridge feather dyed to match body and tied in forward before the head and eyes are added, then pulled back over the head and tied down in front of hackle

Colors: Dark olive-brown, dirty brown, gray-brown, tan-gray, olive-tan

Caddis and alderfly patterns for alpine lakes.
Top: Black Alderfly, Wet and Black Alderfly Dry.
Middle: Alpine Caddis Pupa and Peeking Caddis.
Lower: Bucktail Caddis and Jughead Caddis

organisms on which they feed. These dragonfly nymphs also match their habitat in color, with shades of grayish-tan, brown, olive-brown and olive-tan being common.

Although they don't cause selective feeding on alpine lakes these dragonfly nymphs are readily devoured by cruising trout. Imitations for the mud-dwelling dragons are especially productive when fished to visible trout: As discussed in Chapter 2, allow the fly to settle on the bottom and then just as a trout approaches, "jump" the fly from the mud with a series of two or three quick, short strips.

Scuds, Water beetles, Snails

Alpine trout can on occasion turn selective to water beetles or to scuds (freshwater shrimp). The latter can at times form the critical element in the diet of some stillwater trout. This is rarely the case in alpine lakes simply because most are not rich enough to support dense scud populations. Still, on those few alpine lakes where scuds are abundant they will at

A dragonfly, freshly emerged from its nymphal shuck, dries its delicate wings beside an alpine lake in Oregon.

times trigger selective feeding behavior on the part of the fish.

Scuds look like tiny shrimp: Pick one up and examine it closely and you will find a shrimp-like back and body with numerous tiny legs on the bottom. In the hand scuds often curl into round balls but in the water they dart about with surprising speed and agility.

Most alpine lake scuds are small, often smaller than a No. 16 imitation. But even when the naturals are considerably smaller, a No. 16 or 18 pattern will draw strikes, so I usually don't worry about going any smaller. Scuds vary widely in color but shades of olive, gray, tan and combinations thereof are most common on the high lakes. Specific color need not be a concern. Rather, an imitation that is reasonably close in shade and size and is fished with a series of two- or three-inch darts followed by pauses will usually do the trick. To determine the color, size and approximate density of scuds in a given lake simply turn over a few rocks in the shallows and capture the crustaceans as they dart away.

Water beetles, including backswimmers and water boatmen, can usually be imitated with imprecise patterns as well, my favorite being Soft Hackle Zug Bugs or standard Zug Bugs or any of several easy-to-tie water beetle imitations. While trout may at times feed selectively on these small beetles, the fish rarely turn selective to specific pattern. Use a long leader and retrieve the fly with a series of short, erratic strips along with a few pauses. One easy method for fishing beetles is to employ a fast-sinking line and a weighted imitation that will sink quickly, imitating the

Top: Super Scud (left) and Water Boatman (right) Middle: Taylor Snail.
Bottom: Trueblood Otter Shrimp(left) and Peacock Water Beetle (right).

diving action of a water beetle just returning from a trip to the surface (where they must go for air).

The other choice is to fish a foam-bodied beetle (like the Dancing Water Beetle listed on page 28) on a fast-sinking line. Allow the line to sink while the fly remains on the surface. Then strip the fly a few times (causing a wake on the surface) until it is pulled under. Impart another eight or ten short strips and then allow the fly to float back to the surface. Repeat this procedure until you hook a trout or until you must cast again.

Both scuds and water beetles are most common in fertile lakes and thus may be somewhat insignificant in the diets of trout living in lakes at the highest elevations. However, any lake with extensive weed growth—which, of course, are more common at moderate elevation (e.g. 5 to 7,000 feet)—might well harbor an extensive population of both water beetles and scuds. (Neither water beetles nor scuds require extensive weedbeds but such habitats support the most dense populations.)

Water beetles and scuds prefer shallow water. Scuds often frequent the near-shore margins and are most active during low-light periods. Trout venture into mere inches of water to pursue scuds during the evening and early morning. Similarly, water beetles occur in the greatest densities in water less than four or five feet deep.

The various water beetles are capable of flying in and out of the water, which they do during migrations and during the mating period. They search for prey underwater but must surface to get air. They carry a little air bubble in their hind legs during dives; once this air bubble has been used up the beetles must return to the surface for another.

In most cases, water beetles are eaten opportunistically by alpine trout, the exception being the more fertile lakes where trout might feed on them selectively once in a while. Such selective feeding on water beetles, when I have encountered it in the alpine country, has usually occurred just after ice-out. This is probably a result of the fact that water beetles can and sometimes do remain active all winter at least where they can glean air from hollow pockets in the ice.

A number of years ago Tim Blount and I started tying a floating water beetle pattern in response to an encounter we had on a lake in Oregon: During a calm evening, small water beetles were airborne by the hundreds along the shallow margins of the lake. This being the largest concentration of water beetles we had ever seen flying in and out of the water, we soon noticed that the little insects often encountered substantial difficulty in breaking through the surface film to swim underwater.

In their efforts to penetrate the surface film, the beetles

*Scuds, water beetles and snails
thrive in the shallows of the more fertile
alpine lakes (High Uintas Wilderness, Utah).*

Brook trout, Henry M. Jackson Wilderness, Washington.

would go through all sorts of gyrations, spinning around in quick, tight circles and causing a commotion on the surface that no reasonable trout would ignore. Indeed, the trout went nuts that evening and Tim and I figured out why some people call these water beetles "whirligig beetles." These days, anytime we encounter substantial water beetle activity, we think floating patterns first simply due to the potential for pulse-quickening excitement. Our Dancing Water Beetle (not pictured but pattern listed below) is designed just for those instances.

Snails, like scuds and water beetles, can in some waters occupy a prominent position in the diet of trout. The best snail populations occur in the most fertile lakes so only on occasion will you find an alpine lake loaded with these creatures. Some of the mid-elevation waters (those from 5,000 to 8,000 feet) support substantial weed growth and substantial snail densities.

On such lakes, snails can at times be the dominant trout food: I have cleaned high-lake trout that were stuffed with snails. Snail patterns should be fished near the weedbeds with—naturally—a very slow retrieve. I'm not convinced that the retrieve, no matter how slow, actually mimics the movements of a snail. Instead, I think the movements of the fly attract the trout who then takes the fly because it looks like a snail (or at least looks like something edible).

Leeches

Like most other trout foods, leeches thrive especially well in fertile, weedy lakes. Still, most alpine lakes have at least a token population of leeches with their relative abundance (and significance to trout) increasing proportionally with the amount of weed growth and other organic matter on the lake bed.

Water Beetle, Scud and Snail Patterns

Super Scud
Hook: Wet fly, No. 10-18 (Partridge #SH1)
Tail: A few woodduck fibers
Body: Rabbit fur dubbed with Krystal Flash dubbing loop; picked out
Shellback: Mixture of lemon woodduck fibers and Krystal Flash
Rib: Fine gold wire
Colors: To match natural; olive-gray, pale olive, pink-gray are common

Peacock Water Beetle
Hook: Wet fly, No. 12-16, weighted at front (Partridge #G3A)
Body: Peacock herl
Legs: A few brown partridge fibers on each side of head
Shellback: Peacock herl, lacquered or epoxied

Taylor Snail (Marv Taylor)
Hook: Wet fly, 1X short, No. 8-12 (Partridge #G3A or #A)
Body: Medium dark olive chenille, wrapped over itself to form snail shape
Hackle: One turn dark olive partridge

Trueblood Otter Shrimp
Hook: Wet fly, No. 10-18 (Partridge #G3A)
Tail: Brown partridge fibers
Body: 50-50 mixture of otter and natural cream seal or imitation seal
Throat: Brown partridge

Water Boatman
Hook: Wet fly, No. 10-14, weighted at front (Partridge #G3A or SH1)
Body: Tannish dubbing
Legs: Two brown biots, one per side, tied in at mid-shank
Shellback: Pheasant tail fibers, lacquered or epoxied

Dancing Water Beetle (Shewey)
Hook: Dry fly, No. 12-16 (Partridge #L3A)
Body: Silver tinsel covering hook shank, then pearl Krystal flash tied in at rear and pulled forward. Over the top is a robust piece of dark closed-cell foam, tied in at rear and pulled forward, leaving a large head at front
Legs: Krystal Flash fibers or rubberlegs, tied at front
Note: Though it is impossible to mimic the circular "whirligig" motions of the actual beetle, trout don't seem to care how the fly moves, so long as it trails a wake, which this pattern is designed to do.

Top: Shewey's Nevada Leech. Bottom: Thin-Water Leech.

Leeches are most active during low-light periods and trout rarely pass up an opportunity at such a mouthful: Leeches found in the high lakes can reach lengths of several inches. As a general rule leeches are able swimmers, corkscrewing their ribbon-like bodies through the water with surprising ease. Because of their mode of swimming, leeches demand imitations that provide lots of lifelike movement. Thus marabou patterns and rabbit strip patterns are the rule.

For clear water during daylight hours I usually opt for a pattern I call the Thin-Water Leech. Slender and sparse of dress, the Thin-Water Leech is an imitative pattern designed to closely mimic the swimming leech. When fishing at and after dusk or in colored water, I prefer a more fully dressed leech pattern so I opt for either a Woolly Bugger or a Nevada Leech, which is constructed of Mohair and rabbit strip and offers a more substantial impression.

In either case the leech can be fished in several ways. My favorite retrieve features a series of long (one to two feet), slow pulls imitating the swimming leech and often drawing violent strikes. When fishing is really tough, however, I sometimes crawl a leech ever so slowly along the bottom. Even when every other conceivable fly and method has failed, this deep-fished leech often entices trout to strike.

Leech Patterns

Shewey's Nevada Leech

Hook: 4XL streamer, No. 6-10 (Partridge #CS17 or CS5)
Tail: Short, thin rabbit strip (standard width strips available in fly shops must be split in half down the center to obtain appropriate thickness)
Body: Mohair
Head: Rabbit hair, with guard hairs, spun on thread and wrapped on shank (two-three turns)
Colors: Black, olive, brown, purple, bloodworm red

Thin-Water Leech

Hook: 3XL nymph, No. 6-12 (Partridge #SH3)
Tail: Three to four strands of Krystal Flash then marabou, sparse
Body: Large ostrich herl wrapped on hook shank and trimmed top and bottom
Rib: Fine copper wire, counterwrapped

Note: Hook is bent slightly upward at mid-shank and then a few wraps of lead wire are added to the forward half of the hook; should be fished with an open loop knot to allow maximum free play on the leader.

CHAPTER 4

Float Tubing The Alpine Lakes

A float tube, waders, fins and a pump add a good 10 or 12 pounds to the weight of your pack and often that is weight well spent. Many alpine lakes are highly conducive to float tube fishing, especially some of the larger waters. My general rule of thumb is this: If I plan to visit large lakes or lots of lakes where a reasonably easy hike is required, I take the float tube. If I'm prospecting (traveling fast to sample numerous remote lakes where cross-country travel is the norm) I leave the tube at home.

Of course you have to define a hard hike for yourself. If you've spent some time on the trail already in the past month or so and are in good shape, 8 miles, mostly uphill, might seem a reasonable distance to lug a float tube. On the other hand, I've seen some two-mile hikes that I wouldn't tackle with that extra 12 pounds even when I'm in the best of shape.

I've never seen an alpine lake where I needed a float tube to catch fish but I've seen plenty where the float tube afforded me a real advantage. A tube will allow you to fish back toward shore which can be deadly and it will allow you fish areas beyond reach of the shore. Lake Anne is a pretty little 16-acre gem that rests aside the trail into Oregon's popular Marion Lake. Filled only with pan-sized brookies, Lake Anne is still a lot of fun because it is completely choked with aquatic weeds during the summer and early fall. I can't imagine fishing it without a float tube. The lake is virtually unwadeable because of thick, soft bottom debris.

Tim Blount float tubing a grayling lake in Wyoming's Wind River Mountains.

Tim Blount with a nice grayling taken while float tubing a Wyoming lake.

A float tube allows anglers to fish areas that might not be accessible from shore. Ken Hanley photo.

I found another small lake, well off the nearest trail, that was home to brook trout up to 16 inches—and a fat 16 inches at that. The shoreline around most of the lake was a jungle-like tangle of dense alders and was virtually impenetrable. If that weren't enough, the banks below the alders dropped off to three feet of water, covering a bottom of deep ooze. You couldn't wade in that stuff even if you could get through the alders. Only three places offered access: Two fallen trees large enough to walk out on and fish from and a 20-foot section of shoreline devoid of alders and with a rock bottom. You could catch a few fish from these places but most of the brookies fed farther out in the lake. The second time I visited this lake I was smart enough to take a float tube which I launched from the one open shoreline. That float tube made all the difference.

You will run into lakes like that once in a while. If you have a float tube along you're in business. If not, you could be in for a long day of casting practice. Incidentally, some float tubes are lighter than others. I have a nice big float tube with all the frills that I use on the lowland waters but I'd hate to have to carry it any distance. Thus, I also own a smaller, no-frills (i.e. 16-inch inner-tube, no pockets, no backrest) float tube specifically for long hikes into the high lakes. This particular float tube called the Caddis Ultra-Lite has been made by Caddis Manufacturing since 1981.

Moreover, some float tube manufacturers, most notably Caddis, are now building special air bladders designed to be inflated by mouth. These air bladders are substantially lighter in weight than the traditional rubber inner tubes and you needn't carry an air pump. Thus, with the advent of these air bladder systems you can carry a float tube fully deflated and folded up neatly on or in your pack and then simply blow it up like a pool toy when you reach the lake.

Any time you decide to haul the float tube along, choose your waders with care. A pair of 3 mm neoprene waders will keep you warm a lot longer than a pair of thin nylon waders. Yet the nylon waders take up little room and add little weight to your pack whereas the bulky neoprenes are something of a pain to carry. If you choose nylon waders you won't be able to stay in cold water very long. Again, perhaps the best strategy is to choose waders based on the relative difficulty of the hike. Whenever possible I opt for the neoprenes simply because I can stay in the water a lot longer.

You will need fins as well. Just carry the lightest weight pair you can find. Attach a two-foot piece of duck-cord to each fin so you can strap them to your legs. Losing a fin in the middle of a deep lake on the first day of a week-long venture is a real downer. For inflating inner-tube-style float tubes, carry a small bike pump—the tubular type carried by serious bike riders. These are small pumps so inflating the tube can take a long time (an eternity when fish are rising). Therefore, you might prefer to hike with the float tube strapped to the rear of your pack either fully inflated or partially inflated (the latter when hiking through brush or heavy timber).

Once you are on the water, think about your float tubing approach in strategical terms: Where are the most likely places to find fish and how should you best approach these areas. Typically, I pinpoint inlets first, tubing quietly to within 30 to 60 feet (depending on how clear and shallow the water is and how timid the trout are) of the mouths of any streams running into the lake. If trout are holding at the creek mouths waiting for food to drift to them you can generally get pretty close. On the other hand if trout are actively cruising around near the mouth of the creek, you might opt to stay a little farther back.

The same is true for any good trout cover—shoals, logs, talus, weedbeds, shaded areas, outlets—if the trout are cruising you should move slowly. In shallow water, I prefer to stop paddling and stand up to make the cast. From a standing position I can see into the water better and usually cast more accurately.

The new bladder-system float tubes are a backpacker's dream because they weigh only a few pounds and are designed to be inflated by mouth. The author favors the models produced by Caddis Manufacturing of McMinnville, Oregon because of their super-tough, one piece bladder (pictured is the Caddis Premier Model).

Float tubes lend themselves well to trolling tactics, which can prove invaluable when you are simply searching for trout. Using a fast sinking line and two or three flies, kick gently around the lake or part of the lake, trailing line behind. Plan your trolling route to take you near any likely looking structures including drop offs, talus slides, shoals and weed beds. As you fin about the lake, keep the rod tip underwater so you can feel delicate strikes. Also, use your free hand to constantly manipulate the line with short strips, tugs and releases—this will help animate the flies.

When you hook a fish or feel a strike stop and fish that region thoroughly, using the countdown method to fish different depths. The countdown method works like this: Determine the sink rate of your sinking fly line by reading the literature accompanying its packaging. If that sink rate is, for example, 6 ips (inches per second) then you have to count 20 seconds in order for the line to reach a depth of 10 feet. Remember, however, that your fly line will plane toward the surface when you troll so even on fast-sinking line the strike may have occurred much shallower than you might think. For this reason you should start a few feet below the surface and work to greater depths.

If you don't hook another trout in that area continue trolling. Sometimes you hook fish all day long while trolling and yet never interest one when you stop, cast and retrieve.

CHAPTER 5

Before You Go: Getting In Shape For Alpine Travel

Along hike into an alpine lake basin can be a lot like work if you are not physically prepared. In fact, the misery that many people associate with long, steep hikes is really only a function of conditioning: If you prepare yourself physically for the experience then the backpacking required to fish high lakes is really not much of a problem. On the other hand, tackling the high country when you are out of shape often results in a miserable and tedious venture.

You needn't build yourself into a star athlete to enjoy alpine fishing. Rather, you should simply strive to attain a level of fitness equal to the task. If your alpine lake fishing for the summer is confined to a single three-day trek into the wilderness covering a total of only six or eight relatively flat miles, then you might not need to change your present fitness program at all (assuming you are already a reasonably active individual).

On the other hand, a week-long trek into remote, high-elevation, rugged country, covering lots of miles, or a summer filled with several such adventures requires that you improve your level of conditioning to the point that physical fitness will not pose any kind of barrier to actual travel in the wilderness. Nothing is

Anglers who are well conditioned will find the steep trails and high altitudes much easier going.

*Some of the best alpine lakes are
found in the most inaccessible locations.*

worse than undertaking a ten-mile trek, all members of the party filled with enthusiasm, only to have one person fade at the five mile mark, virtually quit at the eight mile mark and be spent for the next several days of what was supposed to be a 50 mile, week-long fishing adventure.

Before undertaking any physical training routine you should consult a physician. If you are new to physical conditioning, including weight training and cardiovascular training, a complete physical check-up and training consultation with a doctor should be considered mandatory. If you already exercise regularly then you may only need to alter your regiment to specifically train your body for backpacking and hiking.

To shoot all the photos for this book I spent an entire summer and early fall traveling the West and backpacking into various wilderness areas. Having always been physically active, I simply altered my training regiment to prepare for carrying a backpack over steep terrain at high altitudes. The regiment that I followed worked for me; another individual might do something quite different and still attain the desired result of getting in shape for alpine travel. With that in mind let's examine the routine that I used.

Having trained with free weights for eight years I was already fairly strong in many areas but I still wanted to further strengthen my lower back and abdominals. A strong mid-section can eliminate lower back fatigue and pain often associated with carrying a backpack over any appreciable distance. In fact, I think it fair to say that you could develop bulging biceps and a hulking chest and not benefit nearly so much as you would from simply paying a lot of attention to strengthening the lower back and abdominal muscles.

So developing a stronger mid-section was one objective of my new routine. In addition, I felt compelled to increase my cardiovascular fitness,which is undoubtedly the single most important improvement that the average person can make before tackling alpine country. I don't really enjoy running anymore but I decided nonetheless to put in two or three runs a week up until the time that I really started doing a lot of hiking. Virtually all of these runs were in the steep hills near my home although I augmented them with some track work that included timed miles, four or five per workout, all interspersed with quarter mile walks.

When the season arrived for backpacking into high country, I began taking one or two day-hikes per week up until the time of my first extended trip (into the Idaho Sawtooth Mountains). At that point, I was on the road almost continuously for two months and hiking every other day or so. I did not run during this time simply because time was not available. But some of the hikes I took provided grueling workouts on their own and during others I purposely moved at a pace that would provide a good cardiovascular workout. Incidentally, on my pre-season day hikes I carried a large day-pack filled with whatever unnecessary items would add weight.

When time permitted during my travels I sought out the nearest gym and snuck in for a weight-room workout, always complete with abdominal and lower back routines.

In any event, choose whatever cardiovascular fitness program you want so long as you can stick with it. Some options might include several long, brisk walks each week for six or eight weeks; running, whether long or short distances; an aerobics class; or any number of sports that keep your feet moving and your heart working at an elevated level. Your doctor, local fitness club pro or just about any good book on the subject can explain the concept of "training-zone heart rate" which is critical to gaining maximum benefit from your routine.

As important as a good training regimen might be, it will prove inconsequential if your feet don't hold up to the rigors of backpacking. You should use the best footwear you can get; more importantly, your boots should fit perfectly. But even with perfectly suited footwear you still run the chance for blisters if your feet are not well conditioned for hiking.

If you plan to spend any amount of time on the trail you should take pains to toughen the bottom of your feet. Take your shoes off. Walk around the house and yard barefoot as often as possible; spend an hour doing stadium workouts (walking up and down the stairs in a sports stadium) without shoes. Run or walk on the beach barefoot. Better yet, sign up for a martial arts class where you will go barefoot on a hardwood floor. In short, toughen up the bottom of your feet and you'll never need to worry about blisters which can be ruinous to a backpacking venture.

For what it's worth the following weight-training routine is the one that works for me when it comes time to get into peak condition. The routine is based on a three-day rotation, wherein I work a particular muscle group on day one and then work that same muscle group again on day four. If you have never trained with weights before, remember that proper form and execution is the key. The amount of weight you lift is inconsequential when not coupled with good form. Remember also (if you are new to this kind of training) that 10 perfectly executed crunches or back extensions are better than 50 done with improper form.

If a particular exercise asks that you perform 10 reps, then you should use a weight that will enable you to just barely squeeze out those 10 repetitions with no strength left for another rep. When lifting moderate weights (8 to 15 reps per set), I rest for 90 to 120 seconds between sets. With heavy weights (1 to 6 reps) I allow the full two minutes between sets. With a busy schedule many people (myself included) don't have time to work out every day. On those days when time is short, limit the number of sets to three or reduce the number of exercises. Don't feel guilty if a busy schedule prevents you from training for two or three days in a row; conversely, don't make excuses when you do have time to go to the gym.

Day 1 (abdominals, chest, triceps)
Warm-Up

Abdominals: Crunches
Flat Bench Press: 1 set @ 15 reps, 3 sets @ 8 reps, 1 set @ 3-4 reps (total 5 sets)
Incline Press (Barbell): 1 set @ 12 reps, 3 sets @ 7-8 reps, 1 set @ 3-5 reps
Abdominals: Crunches or decline (Roman chair) crunches
Dumbbell Press: 4 sets @ 6-8 reps
Dumbbell Incline Press: 4 sets @ 6-8 reps
Abdominals: Crunches or decline crunches
Tricep Cable Pushdowns: 1 set @ 12-15 reps, 1 set @ 10-12 reps, 3 sets @ 8 reps

Steep, rugged rocky terrain typifies the western alpine country, often demanding that hikers be in top physical shape.

Tricep Barbell Extension: 1 set @ 10-12 reps, 3 sets @ 8 reps
Tricep One-Arm Cable Pushdowns (reverse grip): 4 sets @ 8-12 reps
Abdominals: Crunches
Tricep Dumbbell "Kickbacks:" 4 sets @ 10-15 reps
Stretch: 15-20 minutes

Day 2 (Back, lower back, biceps)

Warm-Up

Lower Back Extension: 50
Wide-Grip Cable Lat Pull (behind head): 1 set @ 15 reps, 4 sets @ 10 reps, 1 @ 8 reps
Seated Rows: 1 set @ 15 reps, 4 sets @ 10-12 reps, 1 set @ 8 reps
Lower Back Extension: 50-100
Narrow-Grip Lat Pulls (reverse grip): 4 sets @ 8-10 reps
Wide-Grip Cable Pulls (to front): 3-4 sets @ 8-10 reps
Standing Bar curls or Preacher Curls: 1 set @ 12-15 reps, 4 sets @ 10 reps
One-Arm Preacher Curls: 4-5 sets @ 8-12 reps
Lower Back Extensions: 50
Optional: Concentration Curls: 3-4 sets @ 8-10 reps
Stretch: 15-20 minutes

Day 3 (Legs, shoulders, abdominals)

Warm-Up Skip rope, ride stationary bike, or similar—10 minutes
Abdominals: Crunches
Squats: 1 set @ 12-15 reps, 3 sets @ 10-12 reps, 1 set @ 8 reps
Military Press: (behind the neck) 1 set @ 15 reps, 3 sets @ 8-12 reps, 1 set @ 6 reps

Lunges: 1 set @ 15 reps, 4 sets @ 12 reps, 1 set @ 8 reps
Shoulder Flies: (side) 3 sets @ 10-12 reps, 1-2 sets @ 8 reps
Dumbbell Shoulder Press: 4 set, @ 6-10 reps
Leg Curls: 4 sets @ 8-15 reps
Leg Extension: 4 sets @ 8-15 reps
Abdominals: Crunches
Stretch: 20-30 minutes

Any of countless other exercises could be substituted for or added to those above. The weight-training specialist at your local gym or club can help you set up a program specifically suited to your needs and can demonstrate proper form and execution for all the exercises. If you intend to undertake a major expedition into the wilderness (a 10-day, 60-mile excursion above timberline, for example) you should take your pre-trip training very seriously, perhaps getting started on strength training as early as six months or more ahead of time and on cardiovascular training at least two months before the outing.

On the other hand a weekend-long venture of just a few miles might not require such serious physical training. Still, any improvement in conditioning makes life on the trail that much more enjoyable.

Finally, if you intend to hike with or lead a group on an extensive wilderness fishing trip, take pains to see that everyone involved does what is needed to get themselves into a state of physical conditioning equal to the task. Work out a schedule that allows members of the group to train together once or more each week for six or eight weeks leading up to the excursion. Working out as a group can be a lot of fun and is easier for many people and once on the trail, the entire squad will reap the benefits of such pre-event training.

CHAPTER 6
Planning Wilderness Fishing Trips

Before you can realistically plan a trip into the wilderness you must decide what exactly you hope to do or find. Do you want big trout? Would you prefer numerous trout over a few large ones? Are you after a particular species, like golden trout or grayling? Do you seek solitude above any particular fishing situation or are you willing to share a lake or lake basin with other people?

You must temper these questions with a realistic assessment of your outdoor skills. After all, a 10-mile trek by compass through heavily-timbered, trail-less terrain requires substantially more know-how than a two-mile walk over a well-used path. Consequently, if you desire to fish remote waters in uncrowded, hard-to-reach areas, you must first acquire the skills needed to access such places.

The most basic of outdoor skills, whether you go to the mountains for a day or for two weeks, is the ability to read a map. Map reading goes beyond simply knowing what road to turn off on and what trail to take. Good maps contain a wealth of useful information for those who know what to look for and are as valuable to the planning stages of a wilderness trip as they are to wilderness travel itself. The following chapter will deal explicitly with map and compass skills for backcountry travel. Here we will concern ourselves with using maps during the planning stages of a high-country fly fishing adventure.

Before planning wilderness fishing excursions you should define your objectives.
If you want big golden trout or grayling like these you must be willing to work.

Large golden trout.

Before you get too serious about the maps, decide on a place to go. Do you want golden trout? Then try Wyoming, Montana or California. Big cutthroat? Try Idaho or Colorado. Big brook trout? Maybe Oregon or Washington. In short, make a few general decisions. Having done that, obtain the maps produced by the U.S. Forest Service (national forest maps and wilderness area maps). The national forest maps in most cases are not topographical, meaning that they do not detail slope and elevation with contour interval lines. Most wilderness area maps sold by the Forest Service are topographical. Except for some of the wilderness area topo maps, these Forest Service maps are of too small a scale to show precise detail (which makes them impractical for cross-country travel) but they help in giving you a general idea of what is available and they show you the roads to follow in getting to a particular trailhead.

When perusing these maps keep your goals in mind. If solitude combined with good fishing is what you hope to find then look for lakes and lake basins that require lengthy hikes or are situated away from trails altogether. Cross-country hikes have led me to some of the best lakes I've ever fished.

After deciding on a few potential destinations, your next step is to make a few phone calls. Start with the state fish and game agency. Getting to the right person might require several phone calls or transfers but you are after two things: The best you can hope for is to locate a staff biologist who has recently visited the lake or lakes in question. That occurrence in this age of helicopter and airplane fish stocking is a rarity. So your next best bet is a biologist or staff person who can look up stocking records for you. You will need the name and location of whatever lakes you intend to ask about. In most states, office personnel can look up stocking records so you won't need to bother a biologist (they

are busy people). Incidentally, stocking records are generally available for public inspection if you are willing to visit your Fish and Game headquarters.

Having ferreted out fish information, call the Forest Service office whose district includes the wilderness area you intend to visit. Addresses and phone numbers for these district offices (along with the regional offices) are listed on the cover of many U.S. Forest Service maps and in Chapter 10 of this book.

Ask the Forest Service personnel if anyone from their office has recently visited the area in question. Ask about snow levels, trail conditions, road conditions leading to the trailhead, specific terrain questions, or anything else that might be pertinent. At times I have asked a ranger to dig out a topo map and go over my intended cross-country route just in case they know of some obstacle that I couldn't discover from the map alone (e.g. "the map doesn't really show it but there is a 30 foot cliff running the length of that ridge—you'd have to go all the way around."). Sometimes I have even found Forest Service people who have fished particular lakes recently and can provide excellent information along those lines.

As you examine fish-stocking records, you are likely to encounter lakes with no history of plantings. Historically, only a tiny fraction of alpine lakes had native fish populations. Those few that did generally contained cutthroat or in a few cases bull trout. Thus, if you find a lake with no official stocking record you can assume it is either devoid of fish or contains naturally reproducing trout (whether native or simply trout of hatchery origins that have managed to establish reproducing populations).

In fact, a district Fish and Game biologist can likely tell you whether a particular unstocked lake holds wild fish or no fish at all. Biologists or stocking records can also tell you what kind of fish are in a given lake. If you learn that a particular water holds naturally reproducing brook trout you stand a good chance of finding these fish to be small and stunted due to overpopulation—a common problem with brookies in high lakes.

On the other hand a lake that is stocked every third or fourth year with brook trout (and where they do not reproduce) might very well offer surprisingly large fish. I found a small lake in Idaho's Selway-Bitterroot Wilderness that contained fat 16-inch brook trout. Later I looked up the stocking history and found that this lake was planted with these trout every five years. I had fished this lake four years after its last stocking. I returned a year later in September when the brook trout don their gorgeous spawning colors and found 17- and 18-inch fish.

Having done your homework with the Fish and Game agency and the Forest Service, your next step is to obtain good topographical maps if they will be needed. For some wilderness areas, the U.S. Forest Service offers good topo maps with ample detail. In many cases, however, the U.S. Geological Survey topo maps (especially the 7.5 Minute series) are invaluable. These USGS maps are available at many sporting goods stores, bookstores and other such places or you can order them directly from the USGS. If you order the maps from the USGS allow a month or so for delivery. The address for ordering maps is as follows:

United States Geological Survey
Map Distribution, Western Branch
Box 25286, Federal Center Bldg. 41
Denver, CO 80225

Topo maps enable you to plan the best routes and also give you some idea of the time required to cover a certain distance. Time your hiking speed at home by measuring an uphill mile on your car's odometer and then walking the same course. Let's say you walk that uphill mile in 20 minutes, add five minutes or so to cover a pace slowed by a heavy pack and by an occasional stop. Add a few more minutes for orientation stops if you intend to travel cross-country (even more in rough or heavily timbered terrain).

Let's assume you identify a cross-country course on your topo map with the route characterized by uneven, heavily-timbered ground. Constant stops to check orientation or to skirt impassable areas may push your pace up to 30 minutes per mile or more. On the other hand if your map shows a trail leading to your destination your travel time will decrease substantially. In any case, first determine your hiking speed and then identify on a topo map those landscape features that will affect your pace. By following this simple procedure you can determine with reasonable accuracy how much time to allow for travel.

Next, study your map for alternatives. Suppose you arrive at a lake only to find it devoid of fish? Alpine lakes are sometimes starved of their oxygen during winter hence killing the trout ("winter kill"). Other times you find a lake overpopulated with stunted trout or full of newly stocked fingerlings.

For these reasons or for whatever other reason you may want to go elsewhere. Such moves will be easier if you have planned a trip that leaves you within a reasonable distance of other lakes. More importantly, do your homework on a number of these other lakes so you know which are likely to hold fish.

In addition to alternative destinations you should study your maps for alternative routes, especially if you intend to travel cross-country. Perhaps a stream swollen by run-off will prove unford-

Sawtooth Mountains, Idaho.

Golden trout.

able; maybe inclement weather will force you to take a lower-elevation course. Whatever the case it pays to have some options.

Finding the "Dream Lakes"

The very best alpine lakes combine total solitude with outstanding fishing. These lakes require you to work: You must work to locate them and then work to get to them. The process of discovering these gems includes the aforementioned research (calling Forest Service and Fish and Game officials) but first you must learn to read topo maps with an eye for potential "dream lakes."

Most of these lakes lay well off the trails; those situated fairly close to trails are usually hidden above, behind or below steep ridges and peaks or are simply hidden from view by other features of the landscape. So, as you peruse the maps consider proximity to trails (or rather the lack of it) to be your first criteria. Then look for relative difficulty: Given two lakes that lie four miles from the nearest trail, the one that is most difficult to reach will be the one least visited.

Incidentally, wilderness area maps produced and sold by the U.S. Forest Service are sometimes better than USGS topo maps for searching out (in your living room, not in the field) hard-to-reach lakes: Many of the USGS topo's for the remote parts of the West are rather dated, having been completed and produced before many of the wilderness areas were even established. Because of their age these maps might not show some of the new trails. I'm a strong believer in cross-referencing between USGS topos and Forest Service wilderness area topos.

To determine difficulty closely examine the contour lines. How steep is the climb? Does the map indicate steep, untimbered slopes that might be talus slides? One of my favorite Wyoming lakes lies only three miles from the nearest trail but is situated some 3,000 feet higher than that trail with 2,000 of those feet accounted for by a mountainside complete with three huge talus slides. Covering those three miles takes half a day.

Another fine lake in Idaho's Sawtooth Wilderness requires one to cross over a high saddle from which the lake is visible

Absaroka-Beartooth Wilderness, Montana.

Seldom-fished "dream lakes" are out there but you must be willing to expend the time and energy to locate and reach them.

below and then circle completely around to the other side of a sprawling glacial cirque before making the descent. Again, the route takes a couple of hours despite the fact that the lake lies just 1,000 feet below the saddle.

Most people just plain won't work that hard, which explains why the quality of the alpine-lake experience increases in direct correlation with the degree of difficulty in reaching a destination.

Having found lakes that fit the criteria of being away from the trails and difficult to reach, your next task is to determine, to the extent possible, the likelihood of finding what you are looking for. Do you want big trout? If so, you should look for lakes situated in places where snow is not likely to accumulate atop the ice cover during winter. It is this snow cover that leads to winter kill: The ice itself is translucent enough to allow sunlight to reach aquatic plant life on the lake bed, but a blanket of snow atop the ice creates an opaque cover through which sunlight cannot pass. When aquatic plant life is starved for sunlight the vegetation soon dies off. Aquatic plants, through the process of transpiration, contribute oxygen to the water. When plants die so goes the oxygen, without which the trout cannot survive.

So, when you study maps looking for those with big-fish po-

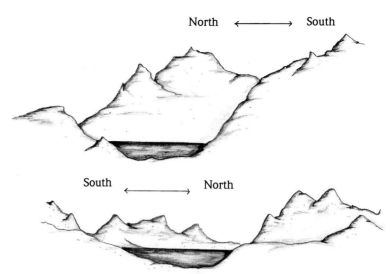

Winter kill: All else being equal, those lakes under the shadow of a north slope and protected from scouring winds (A) will have a greater likelihood of experiencing winter kill than lakes with a southern exposure and lying in the path of scouring winds.

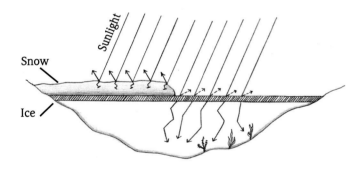

Winter kill is a result of snow piling on top of ice and cutting off light penetration. Without sunlight aquatic plant life cannot photosynthesize and thus cannot contribute oxygen to the water. After a while the lake and its inhabitants are suffocated for lack of oxygen. Those lakes swept free of snow by the wind rarely winter kill because sunlight can pass through the translucent ice cover.

tential pay close attention to the topography of the area and to the general orientation of lakes within that region. Specifically, look for lakes situated directly in the path of prevailing winds or in areas where alpine winds are likely concentrated. A lake that sits high up on the windward side of a bench or saddle, for example, might well be blown clear of snow cover while a lake nestled in a lee well down the other side might accumulate more than its share of snow.

At the same time, pay attention to the general orientation of the lakes. Those located on south slopes benefit from far more sun exposure than lakes hidden on the north side of the mountains. Indeed, if you can find a south-slope lake that is directly exposed to scouring winds you may well find a lake harboring big, healthy trout. In short, a few evenings at home studying your topo maps can make a world of difference once you take to the wilderness.

If you want a particular species, say golden trout or grayling, then you will have to gain access to stocking records or other such information. Call the state Fish and Game and ask about particular lakes. If Fish and Game personnel don't have the time or willingness to look up the information for you, then at least ask them which office you can visit to examine the records for yourself.

In looking over fish stocking information pay special attention to the frequency with which particular lakes are planted with trout (or grayling). A lake that is stocked every year or every other year is probably either fished rather heavily or is prone to winter kill. Conversely, a lake that is stocked every fourth or fifth year might hold some large trout. Also, those waters lacking stocking records or lacking recent stocking records might well hold native trout or healthy, reproducing populations that originated from old plantings (official or unofficial). Such waters might also prove fishless—perhaps stocking efforts just never worked out for one reason or another. In many cases you simply have to go find out for yourself.

Finally, be sure to check with the U.S. Forest Service—specifically the district ranger office responsible for the area in question—to find out about snow conditions. After all, snow fields and snow banks don't show up on topo maps but they can pose a real problem to cross-country travel.

The dream lakes are out there: lots of them. But in most cases you must be willing to do your homework and then do some walking to reach them.

CHAPTER 7

Map & Compass Skills For The Wilderness Traveler

Without question the inability to use map and compass effectively prevents many people from fishing the west's most remote lakes. Working effectively with contour maps and compass allows anglers to find and fish lakes that might only see visitors once or twice a year or in some cases only a few times in the last decade. Moreover, confidence in orienteering skills allows anglers to circumvent the trail systems when it makes sense to do so.

While I've caught some big trout in easy-access lakes, my most memorable trips—those combining solitude with the discovery of large fish in some distant gem of a lake—have required that I travel cross-country to reach my destination. Certainly an understanding of and ability to read contour maps can facilitate much of this kind of travel. But the addition of compass skills allows you to find even the smallest of lakes in the most unreadable of terrain.

Map reading begins at home in the planning stages of your wilderness fishing trip. As described in Chapter 6 you should closely examine good topo maps looking for out-of-the-way lakes in remote areas. Without question the USGS 7.5 Minute series topo maps are best for the wilderness traveler. These maps show a scale of 1:24,000 which means one inch on the map equals 24,000 inches of real distance. More practically, this translates to one inch on the map equating to 2,000 feet.

The USGS office in Denver can provide you, free of charge, with an index map of any western state showing the names and locations for all contour maps available for that state. From this index map (which most retailers of USGS maps have on hand as well) you can determine exactly which 7.5 Minute maps you need. (Incidentally, if you cannot purchase the maps from a bookstore or outdoor store you should contact the USGS well ahead of time as they can take quite a while to fill orders).

Carefully examine the contour map for the best possible route to your destination. Most cross-country routes begin on the trail systems taking advantage of those foot paths that get you as close as possible to your objective. Having located such a trail you must then decide on a cross-country route leaving from that trail. In doing so, read the map carefully: How steep is the terrain? Will you have to cross soggy meadows, rivers or other obstacles?

Obviously, if you are to plan the most efficient route from point A to point B you must be proficient in the art of reading topo maps. Map-reading proficiency begins with familiarizing yourself with all the symbols used to depict different terrain features and man-made features. The USGS can provide you, free of charge, with a complete key or "legend" to all the symbols used on its topo maps.

Naturally, the map's contour lines are especially significant for cross-country travel because they show the size and steepness of the terrain. But these contour lines cannot tell us everything and what they don't say can at times be more significant than what they do say. A 30-foot cliff or steep-sided, 20-foot-deep ravine may not show up on a map with 40 foot contour intervals. Moreover, the contour lines cannot tell us what kind of ground to expect: Will we encounter loose shale or talus or will we find solid rock or tightly-packed earth?

A contour line, in fact, represents the shape and attitude of the terrain only at specified intervals. What lies between these intervals might be entirely different and completely unrepresented on the map.

In addition, cross-country travelers should be aware of the concept of slope error. Slope error simply refers to the fact that a straight line drawn from point A to point B on your map does not give a true measure of distance because it fails to consider the added distances from going up and down slopes.

Take the following example: In the figure below, the straight line at the top represents the line we might draw on our

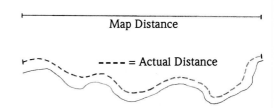

Map distance can vary considerably from actual distance when a lot of up and down hiking is required: If we were to straighten the actual distance line on this diagram it would be substantially longer than the map distance line.

map when planning a route. But in cross section we can see that our hike will include plenty of up and down. Each time we deviate from a perfectly horizontal route we add to the straight line "map distance."

Slope error is given a comprehensive treatment in Robert L Mooers Jr.'s *Finding Your Way In The Outdoors*. The basic principle is simple enough though, as is the practical value of understanding slope error: 10 miles of map distance might be considerably longer if you go up and down a lot along the route, so you may want to adjust your itinerary accordingly.

Remember also that a topo map is really a snapshot in time, making no allowance for changes wrought by man or nature. Your topo map cannot tell you that your route is buried in three feet of snow or that the little brook you must cross is actually swollen to epic proportions by run-off. Only your own experience and the thoroughness with which you pursue local information will indicate those changes in the landscape that are not reflected on a topo map.

So seek local information before ever finalizing your route plans. Call the Forest Service Ranger District office for that area and ask to talk with someone familiar with the wilderness. Ask that individual to dig out a copy of his or her topo map and go over the route together. Sometimes the forest ranger will suggest an alternative route or tell you of an old, unmaintained trail that does not appear on the maps; other times the Forest Service people can warn you of snow levels and stream crossings. Half an hour or so spent on the phone can save a lot of headaches once you get to the trailhead.

The Orienteering Compass

If you intend to pursue cross-country travel in the wilderness (or any wilderness travel), purchase a Type 3 orienteering compass such as the Silva model diagramed below. Then familiarize yourself with all its parts as follows.

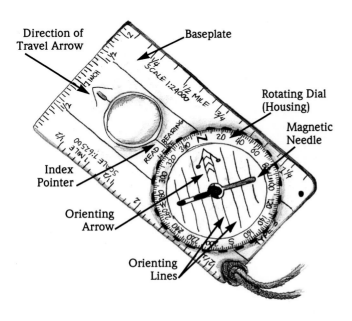

The orienteering compass and its parts.

Declination and Route Planning

Proficiency with map and compass should be considered mandatory for wilderness travelers. With a compass and the skills to use it you can find lakes and streams that rarely see anglers, you can pinpoint your position just about any time and when necessary, you can find your way back to a trail, road, lake or parking lot. In short, orienteering skills allow you to appreciate more fully the wilderness areas of the West because you are unencumbered by the need to stay on the trails.

Various schools of thought persist on how best to teach and use compass skills: My original training occurred in the Cascade Mountains of Oregon where large expanses of evergreen forest, for miles unobstructed by visible landmarks, hide countless small lakes. In those environs, where everything looked pretty much the same and where the lakes often spanned only a few surface acres, accuracy in cross-country travel was at a premium. The price for inaccurate compass work was to pass right by a lake only to start wondering some time later just where the hell I was and how I could have missed the lake.

Thus comes the idea of magnetic declination. Time after time I read magazine articles that explain how to use a map and compass but do so without mention of declination. I believe the opposite approach makes imminently more sense: Explain the merits of correcting for magnetic declination first and then get on with teaching how to follow a compass course. In doing so one automatically learns compass skills that will prove more accurate.

Imagine accurately following a compass bearing for a mile or two and yet still ending up several hundred yards off course. That's enough error to take you right past a small lake (or past your car, the parking lot or your campsite). This is exactly what can occur if you fail to correct for declination. So what is declination? In essence, it is the variation, measured in degrees of latitude, between true geographic north and the place where your compass needle, attracted by the gravitational pull near the North Pole, actually points. On a full circle of 360 degrees, depicted on your compass dial, this variation (in the West) ranges anywhere from 11 or 12 degrees (central Colorado) to 21 or 22 degrees (northern Washington). Simply stated your compass needle doesn't really point to true north.

Meanwhile, your topographic map is situated to true north. In other word, your map speaks one language (true north) while your compass speaks another language (magnetic north). In the interest of accuracy, both map and compass should speak the same language. In order to bring this about you must correct for declination. Of the several ways to do this perhaps the most reliable and easiest is to simply draw magnetic north lines on your topo map.

Some books suggest that you simply draw (with the aid of a straight-edge) a line extending from the magnetic north diagram on the bottom of the maps. But the USGS itself cautions against this method because the graphical illustration of the declination on a given map is just that: An illustration that may or may not actually represent the real value of the actual declination.

Instead, you can use your compass for drawing magnetic north lines ("magnetic meridians") on your topo map. This is done by using the compass as a protractor as follows:

Correcting for Declination by Adding Magnetic Meridians (Lines) to the Map

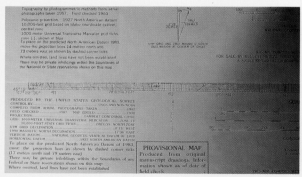

Step 1: On the bottom margin of your topo map find the declination for the area covered on that map. On most USGS topo maps you can read the declination from the graphical representation (to the right of the fine print in this photo). On newer maps the magnetic declination arrow has been omitted from the graphic so you have to read the fine print to find the degrees of declination. The bottom map in this photo shows a new map, where declination is listed amongst the fine print in the lower left corner. Because declination changes over time be sure to check with the USGS to get up-dated declinations if your map is more than 10 or 12 years old.

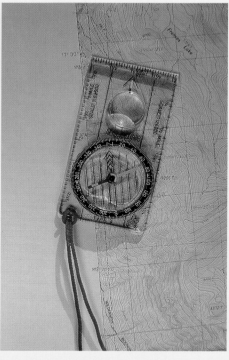

Step 2: Set your compass to the declination by rotating the dial until the appropriate number is aligned with the index pointer. In this example, the declination is about 17 degrees east. In the Western U.S., declination is always east, so you simply add the number of degrees of declination to zero when setting the compass—in other words, east declination means that with the compass set at zero you will turn the dial to the left to set the declination.

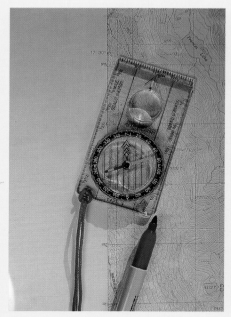

Step 3: Now set the compass on the map so that the orienting lines on the bottom of the housing are parallel to one of the north-south longitude lines on the map or with the map's right or left hand margin. Trace the long edge of the compass with a pen, making certain that the orienting lines remain parallel to the edge of the map or to the north-south meridians. You have now drawn a magnetic north meridian on the map.

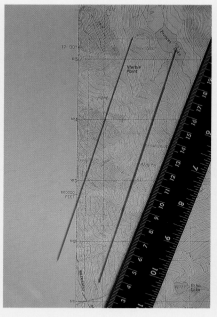

Step 4: Extend this line using a straight-edge taking great care to keep the line straight and true. Then make lines parallel to this one, each spaced by an inch or so.

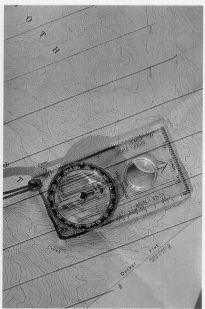

Step 5: Double check the lines with the compass to make sure they are accurate. You needn't line the entire map if your travels are to be confined to just one section of that area.

Taking a Bearing With the Compass

Step 1: Before you can take a bearing you must orient the map to give a true directional picture of the land. To do this, first set the compass housing at exact north and then place the compass on the map so its long edge is parallel to one of the magnetic north lines. Then rotate map and compass together until the red north end of the compass needle is perfectly boxed inside the orienting arrow inscribed on the bottom of the housing. Your map is now oriented.

Step 2: Now lay the compass on the map so its long edge touches both your starting point and your destination (A and B, respectively in this photo).

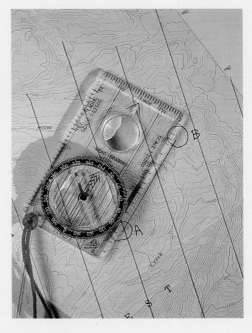

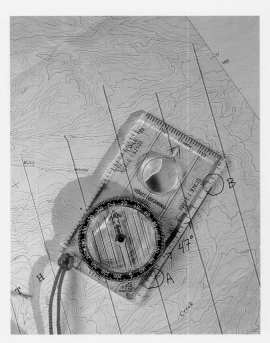

Step 3: Holding the compass baseplate firmly in position rotate the housing until the red north end of the compass needle is boxed in the orienting arrow. The number now at the index pointer (47 degrees in this example) is your bearing. I make a habit of circling and labeling my starting point and my destination, tracing a straight line connecting the two and writing the bearing, along with directional arrows, on the line.

1. Set the compass dial to the declination indicated at the bottom of the topo map, 17 degrees east in our example.

2. Now place the compass on the map so that one of the orienting lines on the bottom of the dial is perfectly aligned with either the right or left map margin or with a longitude line (north-south) on the map.

3. Holding the compass firmly in place and using either the left or right side of the baseplate as a straight-edge, draw a line the length of the baseplate.

4. Using a straight-edge, draw lines parallel to the first one, each spaced by about an inch.

After completing these lines on the map you can forget about declination. By using the drawn-in magnetic meridians you automatically compensate for declination (which is always easterly in the American West).

Bear in mind that declination is not constant and changes slowly over the years. Thus some of our old USGS topos have outdated declination values. To check on current declination you

Eagle Cap Wilderness, Oregon.

can contact the USGS and ask for a declination chart or for change values. Or you can determine declination yourself for a given location by using Polaris, the North Star (or other methods which are explained in the compass/orienteering guides listed at the end of this chapter).

In any case, now that you have corrected for declination by lining the map with magnetic north lines, you are ready to plan your actual route while still in the comfort of your living room. Essentially, this is a five-step process as follows:

1. Locate the access routes to the area you intend to visit. Consult a state highway map so you know how to get to the area and then consult a national forest map to show you how to get to the place from which you intend to start.

2. On your topo map locate both your starting point and your destination. If you wish, you can draw a straight line on the map connecting these two points.

3. Now study the topo map to determine the best route to take you from your starting point to your destination. This is where your ability to interpret map symbols comes in handy. If possible, plan the route to take advantage of easy-to-find reference points like peaks, lakes, streams and trails. Bear in mind that, at times, following a stream up to a lake might make more sense than bushwhacking a cross-country compass course through heavy timber. In fact, following portions of streams and segments of trails where they lie along the route can sometimes make the entire route more efficient.

Bear in mind that streams flowing over steep terrain can make for miserable-creek following because such streams over the years have often carved themselves out a steep-sided, waterfall-laden, debris-ridden ravine.

4.   Having determined a probable route, plan individual seg-

ments that combined will get you to your destination.(At this point I like to take compass bearings for each segment, writing these down on the map: The procedure for doing this follows this section.)

5. Study your route with an eye for potential campsites keeping in mind such concerns as proximity to a water source, protection from weather, slope, etc.

Using the Compass

A compass direction, called a "bearing," is expressed in degrees based on a circle of 360 degrees. North is at 360 degrees. East is at 90 degrees; South at 180 degrees; West at 270 degrees. All points on the compass from 0 degrees all the way around to 360 degrees are expressed as bearings and can be used to indicate any direction of travel.

To take a bearing from your map (to determine a direction expressed as a bearing) you must first orient your map and compass to the actual layout of the land. Having already corrected for magnetic declination by drawing magnetic north lines on the map, you can proceed as follows:

1. Set the compass dial to 360 degrees (North) by rotating the dial until N is precisely at the index pointer.

2. Lay the compass on the map with the left or right edge of the baseplate precisely lined up with one of the magnetic north lines that you drew on the map.

3. Rotate map and compass together until the red (North) end of the compass needle is directly aligned inside the orienting arrow on the bottom of the rotating dial. Your map is now oriented and thus gives an accurate directional description of the actual landscape.

With the map oriented, you are now ready to take a bearing for cross-country travel. To do this, proceed as follows:
1. Lay the long edge of the compass baseplate along your intended line of travel so that it touches both the starting point and the destination.
2. Rotate the compass housing until the orienting arrow is aligned with the magnetic north lines. The number on the dial at the index pointer is your bearing.

Traveling by Compass

Having determined the compass bearing that will take you from point A to point B, your next task is to follow that bearing and actually arrive at your destination. This is done by "sighting," wherein you choose an object along your line of travel (along your bearing) and walk to it.

First, however, you must orient your body to face and then walk in, the direction indicated by your bearing. To do this, first set the compass at the appropriate bearing by turning the dial until the correct number is aligned with the index pointer, where the baseplate is inscribed with the words "READ BEARING HERE." In other words, if your bearing is 250 degrees, then turn the dial until 250 is aligned with the index pointer.

Now hold the compass level and in front of you at about mid-torso, with the direction of the travel arrow pointing straight ahead. Slowly rotate your body by shifting your feet until the red end of the compass needle is aligned with the orienting arrow. Raise your eyes and look straight ahead in the direction indicated by the direction of travel arrow. You are now looking in the direction you will travel.

Next choose an object that is directly in line with your bearing. Do this by imagining an extension of the direction of travel arrow that runs straight across the landscape on your bearing until it hits the furthest object you can see and will be able to see from any point along this line.

This object, whether it be a tree, a rock, a bluff, a peak or whatever, must be visible the entire time you are walking toward it. Conversely, the place from which you started should itself be visible the entire time you are walking to the "sighted" object. In open country you might need only a few sightings to reach your destination (e.g. starting point to bluff, bluff to cliffs, cliffs to big dead snag, big dead snag to destination). In heavy timber (or in bad weather) you might have to sight on individual trees only 40 or 50 yards apart and thus make many individual sightings to reach your objective.

The sight line connecting your starting point and your sighted object is sometimes called a "point line." This point line should be and generally is "the longest straight line sighting distance over which two identifiable reference points can be kept in view." (Mooers, *Finding Your Way In The Outdoors*).

The idealized picture of a point line would look like diagram 1., wherein a single sighting line takes you from start to destination.

In the field, a route will be composed of more than one point line. After all, if you can see your destination from your starting point, and from anywhere in between the starting point and the destination, then you certainly would not need a compass to get there. Thus a typical route composed of numerous

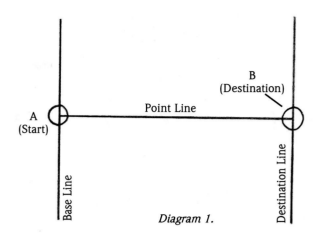

Diagram 1.

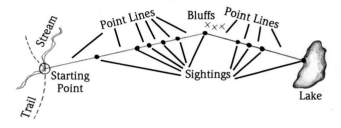

Diagram 2.

Cross-country compass travel is composed of point lines. Diagram 1 above illustrates the idealized version of a point line. In reality, as shown by diagram 2, a cross-country route will be composed of numerous individual point lines. Each point line represents a starting point, the next sighting (sighted object) and the straight line distance between the two.

point lines might look like diagram 2.

This idea of following point lines is crucial to accurate travel along a bearing: You must sight a reference point and walk to it all the while being able to see both the sighted reference point and the starting point. Then you must repeat the procedure again and again until you reach your destination.

Compass Following

Failure to orient your movements to a specific object results in what is termed "compass following." Compass following, typically combined with the apparent human inability to walk a straight line for very long, results in lateral drift from your intended line of travel. The problem often starts when a hiker takes a "field bearing" by pointing the direction of travel arrow on the compass at some visible object, orienting the compass, and then proceeding in that direction without using sightings.

At some point the hiker looses sight of the object on which he took a bearing so he checks with his compass, sets himself to its bearing again and continues. Each time the hiker senses that he might be veering off course he again checks the compass and realigns his walking with the bearing. Invariably between compass checks he starts to drift away from a straight line. The cumulative effect can be a huge error as shown in diagram 3.

Wind River Mountains, Wyoming.

The critical mistake in compass following is the failure to take sightings on objects that remain visible. The orienteer sights an object along the appropriate bearing and then proceeds to that object; the compass follower simply consults his compass and tries to walk in the direction the arrow points. In other words, compass followers try to walk in the direction indicated by a bearing but not toward any specific visible objective along that bearing.

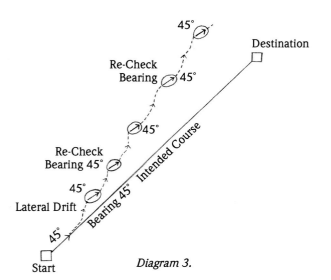

Diagram 3.

Compass following, the result of trying to walk a bearing without reference to sighted objects (i.e. no point lines), results in lateral drift from the intended course. Continued over any distance, compass following generally means missing the destination completely.

What the compass follower should have done was take a bearing on his objective (in the field or on the map) and then follow point lines between sighted objects along that bearing until he arrived at the destination. Remember, all travel by compass must be in reference to two objects: The one in front and the one directly behind.

Landscape Following

Because most alpine areas, more or less by definition, are sparsely timbered, cross-country travelers can often combine compass courses with "landscape travel." Landscape travel simply means that you can identify prominent landscapes by checking them against the topo map and simply guide your movements by these visible features. An example would be a hike across an alpine lake basin where the lakes are clearly visible from any and all vantage points and where the surrounding peaks and ridges are never hidden by trees or other obstructions.

In short, landscape travel is like the ideal point line: A single sighting from A to B. Naturally, you don't need a compass to walk a line between two objects when both are visible and remain visible during the entire route.

But be cautioned: Landscape traveling is no substitute for accurate compass and map work. Use your compass when you need to and walk between landscape features when appropriate. Many cross-country routes are in fact combinations of compass travel and landscape travel.

Other Map and Compass Skills

Proficiency with map and compass will allow you absolute freedom of movement in the wilderness simply because getting lost is impossible. That is not to say you always know exactly

Alpine Angler

where you are, but at the very least you will know where you came from, where you are going and how to figure out where you are.

Cross sectioning, for example, is one technique that can help you determine where you are at a given time. A cross section, or cross bearing, is simply a bearing taken on an object off your point line. The intersection of that bearing and the bearing on which your are traveling tells you your location. This technique, along with several other techniques in orienteering, are fully explained in any of several books on the subject. Among the best are:

Kjellstrom, Bjorn
Be Expert With Map and Compass
Charles Scribner and Sons, New York, 1976 edition

Mooers, Robert L. Jr.
Finding Your Way In The Outdoors
Popular Science Publishing Co., 1972

Kals, W.S.
Land Navigation Handbook, The Sierra Club Guide to Map and Compass
Sierra Club Books, San Francisco, 1983

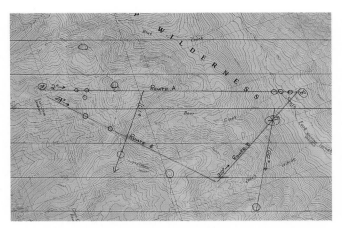

Proficiency with map and compass allows you absolute freedom of movement in the wilderness without anxiety about getting lost. In this scenario an angler might decide to abort his or her planned route A in favor of having a look at an unnamed little lake that lies well off the nearest trail. Thus route B becomes the new plan. A wilderness traveler competent in the use of topo map and compass can use whatever route will take him or her from point A to point B without regard for sticking to the trail system.

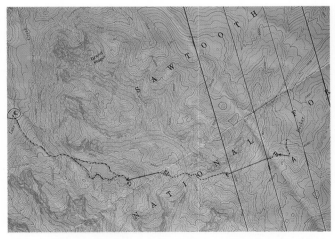

A typical cross-country route in alpine country often combines compass travel with simple landmark travel (walking from visible landmark to visible landmark). In this example, I found the point where the stream crosses the trail and then I followed the stream a short distance to lake A. From there I proceeded by compass a short distance to lake B. Then I followed the outlet of lake B to its confluence with the main stream. Crossing the stream I oriented my map and took a bearing on a peak situated in front of the saddle I intended to cross. I followed that bearing by sighting on individual trees but emerged above timberline a short distance later. From there I could plainly see the peak I was shooting for so I simply took the easiest route to its flank. With my entire route visible before me, I picked my way over very steep ground until I reached the top of the gap between two high peaks. From there, lake C was clearly visible and obviously would be the entire distance down the slope. From lake C, I followed a bearing to lake D. Then I chose the easier of the two shorelines and followed the shore and then the outlet stream until I hit the trail (E).

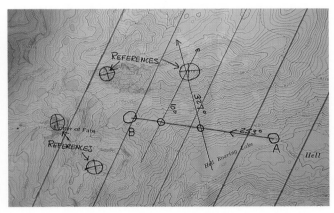

Cross sectioning allows you to determine your progress while following a compass course along a point line. In this example, imagine you are walking the bearing 253 degrees and are intent on reaching the lake marked "B." Your progress has been rather slow so you wonder how much farther you must go to reach the lake. You take a field bearing of 327 degrees by sighting on a visible peak (your reference point). Leave the compass set at 327 degrees. Now orient your map and place the compass on the map so the long edge of the baseplate touches both your point-line (which should be drawn on the map) and your reference (the peak). Keeping the compass touching the reference point, rotate the base of the compass along your point-line until the compass needle is boxed in the orienting arrow. That point, or intersection, where the long edge of the baseplate intersects your line of travel is your approximate location. Thus the intersection of your 253 degree bearing and the 327 degree bearing to the reference point tells you your location. Farther along you could again check your progress in this manner by using the same reference point or any other visible landmark (generally speaking, the closer the reference object is to being at a right angle to your line of travel the more accurate will be your cross-section.)

CHAPTER 8
Wilderness Travel Tips

At The Trailhead

The trailheads of our Western wilderness areas have undergone a remarkable transformation: Not too many years ago one could leave the vehicle, even unlocked, with all sorts of extra outdoor gear inside and wander off into the wilderness for a few days without a second thought. Those days are gone now. Perhaps there exist no "good" thieves, but surely those who break into vehicles at trailheads and other far-off-the-beaten-path outdoor locales are the lowliest of their kind.

Indeed such is the reality today. More and more people are returning from their adventure into the wilderness only to find that their vehicle has been broken into (in some cases stolen altogether). Short of lynch-mob vigilantism the only prevention is the kind of common sense that until recently we needed not worry about: Don't leave any valuables in the vehicle, attach a locking device to the steering wheel, remove the distributor cap and so on.

The other changes affecting our wilderness areas are less troublesome: More and more wilderness areas around the West require that you register before entry. In many cases wilderness registration is a do-it-yourself process at the trailhead where you simply sign in and go about your business. In a few places, however, you need a permit from a Forest Service office. Be sure to call the Forest Service ahead of time to check on such details.

Many trailheads are located at or near campgrounds allowing for the possibility of "base camping" whereby you plan a week's stay at the campground and make one-and two-day excursions to different lakes in the wilderness. Base camping allows you to travel light and fast so you can sample any number of lakes over the course of a day or two. This is a great way to scout for wilderness lakes and lake basins to which you might like to return for a longer stay in the future.

Backpacking Equipment

Comfortable backpacking starts with the feet: Get good boots and break them in before taking to the high country. My preference is for the light-or medium-weight hiking boots that have gained a tremendous following in recent years. I put a pair

An ideal campsite in Wyoming's Bridger Wilderness.

Alpine anglers must often cross steep talus slides and boulder fields to reach the most remote lakes. "Walk with your eyes" by planning your steps ahead of time, test each foothold and maintain three points of contact (e.g. two feet and a hand or two hands and a foot) at all times.

Trailheads can be crowded these days and car break-ins are on the increase in many such places. Take all due precautions to prevent your vehicle from being broken into or stolen outright.

of Danner boots, which are constructed of leather and Gortex material, through a couple hundred on- and off-trail miles along with two bird-hunting seasons and they held up to all of it (believe me, chukar hunting has a way of eating boots).

Socks should be chosen with care. Start with a pair of lightweight polypro socks underneath and then add a pair of heavy wool-blend boot socks. I've never had a blister but that good fortune is more a matter of foot conditioning than anything else.

As discussed in Chapter 5, anyone planning to spend considerable time on the trail should begin toughening up his or her feet well ahead of time. Take a martial arts class that requires you to work out barefoot on a hard floor; walk or run barefoot in the sand or on a track; do stadium workouts barefoot or sign up for a sand volleyball league. Do whatever it takes but toughen your feet. Few people take the time to do so and many of them suffer as a consequence. I've known people to go to great lengths to condition themselves physically for wilderness travel only to be bogged down by blisters because they neglected to toughen the feet.

On the trail or off-trail in open country, I usually hike in heavy cotton shorts. In brush or in snow I wear a pair of military-style field pants (the baggy kind with multiple pockets and cuffed legs). On top I wear a T-shirt under a heavy cotton or

A base camp set up at a campground located near a wilderness border. From such a basecamp you can make a series of one-day hikes into various lakes.

quilted cotton shirt. I can easily remove the outer layer when I get too warm.

No matter what you wear while hiking, keep your rain gear handy. Sudden rain or snow showers, not to mention full-fledged storms, can occur with little warning in the high country. I prefer an actual rubberized rain suit, which at least for me has proven more reliable than expensive Gortex jobs and the like. In addition, I carry a large, sturdy, plastic garbage bag that will fit over my entire pack during wet weather.

External-frame backpacks, incidentally, offer distinct advantages over internal-frame models. For starters, you can lash just about anything (including rod tubes, float tubes, fins, etc.) to the frame. Also, with the frame suspending the payload slightly away from your body, hard items inside the pack won't be jabbing you in the back all day.

Dressed for the trail—Wind River Range, Wyoming.

I also hike with a fanny pack, wearing it in the forward position so I can easily reach handy items kept inside, including sunscreen, insect repellent, map, compass, pocket knife, extra matches and tackle items.

The aforementioned sunscreen and insect repellent are mandatory. I use Muskol containing nearly 100 percent Deet (the active ingredient). Because Deet is reportedly quite toxic (as one would certainly expect) I have gone to using standard Muskol (40 percent Deet) on my face. Never make the mistake of forgetting the bug dope: I've seen high-country mosquitos and black flies drive folks out of the wilderness and right back to the city.

As for sunscreen, I use at least 25-SPF because UV rays are more intense at high elevation. I also carry sunblock (zinc) for my nose. Good polarized sunglasses, of course, are a necessity in fending off glare from snowfields, lakes and sheer rock faces (and to help spot fish in the water). You will also want a brimmed hat. I wear a durable military-style "boonie hat" that provides adequate sun protection and is low maintenance. I also carry a warm stocking cap, which can be a real life-saver on cold alpine nights and mornings.

Sleeping Bags and Tents

Good backpacking bags—those that combine ample warmth with little weight—tend to be expensive but a good bag is really one of the most important items for alpine camping. My synthetic-fill bag weighs six pounds, which is rather heavy by a backpacker's standards. I've never been cold in that bag and I only paid $150 for it as opposed to super-light-weight bags, offering the same warmth factor, that sell for $300 to $500.

Any number of synthetic fill materials are on the market today. If you go that route, choose the best you can afford. That means reasonably light in weight and plenty warm. Bags rated anywhere from below zero to about 15 degrees will keep you comfortable during those frosty alpine nights.

Down-filled bags have the distinct advantage of compressing down to less cumbersome sizes than their synthetic-filled counterparts, but you must keep down sleeping bags dry. So long as you can indeed keep them dry, down bags are excellent, albeit expensive, sleeping bags. Whatever your choice in filling (synthetic or down), mummy-style bags provide better heat retention than rectangular models.

Along with a good, warm sleeping bag you want some sort of ground pad to go underneath. The Therma-rest pads, which virtually self-inflate, are a great investment. A simple foam pad weighing next to nothing is your next best alternative.

Lastly, you want some kind of tent or other shelter. I carry a simple dome-style tent complete with a rain canopy that is simple to erect and weighs only a few pounds. During clear nights when mosquitos are not a problem, I usually skip the tent and sleep under the stars. But when inclement weather threatens or when a deranged swarm of biting bugs are on the war path, I'm always glad I packed the tent along.

Often I trade the tent for a large, heavy-plastic drop cloth and enough duckcord (a strong woven twine used to attach weights to decoys) to set up a simple shelter just about anywhere with the help of a few trees. This light-weight, easy-to-pack arrangement has proven versatile on many a wilderness trip but I always take the tent during the early and late part of the season when mountain weather, which is never terribly reliable, can change on a whim.

If you go this route, pre-cut the duckcord into four 12-foot lengths and two 20-foot lengths. The shorter lengths will tie off to the corners of the drop cloth (or you can get metal clips to attach to the tarp) while one or two long pieces of duckcord will serve as a center rope over which you will drape the tarp. Don't forget to pack a half dozen light-weight tent stakes. The same equipment can be formed into a lean-to type shelter or several other designs.

The aforementioned metal clips that you can use to attach cord to a drop cloth are available at stationery and office supply stores. They are called binder clips and come in a variety of sizes.

Before buying them, however, test each one by attaching it to a single sheet of thin paper and pulling. Ideally, the paper should rip before the clip slides free thus assuring a solid grip on the drop cloth out of which you will form a shelter.

Cooking in the High Country

Most if not all of your high-country cooking should be done over a backpacking stove such as the ever-popular Coleman Peak series stove, which run on white gas. A stove burns more reliably than a fire fed by pine or fir at 10,000 feet and offers the added advantage of not harming the soil whose nutrient base takes hundreds of years to rebuild after being torched.

That is not to say you can't build a fire. Many wilderness travelers are entirely against the idea but I've been warming hands, socks, Pop Tarts, coffee and numerous other items over small fires in the backwoods since I was nine years old and on

Coleman backpacking stove and fuel bottle.

the loose in Idaho's Caribou Mountains. Besides, man has enjoyed the warm glow of a fire for eons and I feel I'm entitled to the same right so long as I build and douse my fires responsibly.

Fires should be small and unobtrusive. If you want a fire look for an existing fire ring near your campsite and use it—building a new ring within proximity of an old one is just plain silly, but such actions seem to prevail in some wilderness locales.

When no pre-built ring exists and I want a fire, I build small "pit fires" whereby I cut away the first several inches of duff (the top layer of needles, leaves, etc.) from the ground and place it aside to be replaced later. Then I dig out about eight inches of

Wilderness travelers are encouraged to use backpacking stoves rather than fires.

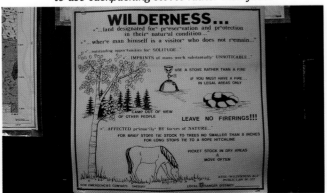

soil, again placing the material nearby so I can return it to the hole when I'm finished. My fire pits run about eight inches in circumference and if at all possible I burn dead, dry hardwood like mountain mahogany, alder, vine maple or aspen.

I allow the fire to burn itself to ashes when I'm done and then I thoroughly douse the remains with water: Pour water on, stir the coals and ashes and repeat as many times as needed until I can bury my hand in the ashy muck and feel nothing but cold water. Then I replace the soil and finally the sod layer. One afternoon rain shower and I defy anyone but the most experienced

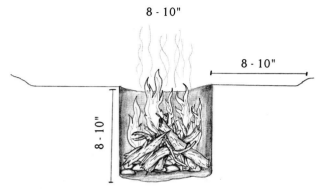

The pit fire. Using a plastic trowel, cut away a 24 to 30 inch diameter piece of sod and set aside to be replaced later. Then scoop out an eight or 10 inch deep hole for the fire. This hole should be about as big in diameter as it is deep. Build the fire in the small pit. A lightweight backpacker's cooking grill is ideal for cooking over such a fire.

of outdoor trackers to find the remains of such a fire. (Incidentally, some wilderness areas or parts thereof have fire restrictions in place during all or part of the season—be sure to check with the Forest Service.)

If you cook over a fire, a light-weight aluminum backpacker's grill is priceless. Such grills occupy very little space and weight in your pack and are perfectly suited to the aforementioned pit-style fires because they are long enough to span the entire hole and support the weight of whatever cooking vessel you use. In addition, you need a plastic trenching tool, which you can buy at a backpacking store for a few dollars.

Also, a folding belt knife with a saw blade will prove invaluable in cutting wood to appropriate lengths for your fire pit. I also carry a tinder kit regardless of whether I intend to build a fire. My favorite tinder is good old-fashioned dryer lint, which you can harvest from the lint screen in your dryer. This highly flammable lint compresses remarkably well and you can stuff an inordinate amount in a plastic film canister. When you can't find dry tinder, this lint material can save the day.

The U.S. Forest Service recommends that wilderness travelers tear apart old fire rings by scattering the rocks about. I've scattered my share but every time I return to those places, a new fire ring has invariably popped up. Thus I have mixed feelings about this practice of helping dismantle fire rings—perhaps in all but the most remote areas we are better off leaving the fire rings to encourage people to use them instead of building new ones.

Regardless, don't leave home without a backpacking stove. They are superior to a fire for cooking, they are quick and efficient and they are comparatively clean. Don't forget extra fuel, which you can carry in special fuel bottles available at most outdoor stores and bring along a tiny plastic funnel for refilling your stove.

Handy utensils include matches in a waterproof vessel; spoons (forks are generally unnecessary); a large, shallow plastic cup, which will serve as your plate and bowl; a small plastic beverage cup for coffee, milk, juice or whatever; one smallish cooking pot along with a small, light-weight skillet if your menu requires it; a small flashlight so you can actually see when you are burning the hell out of dinner; a hand towel (combination pot holder/dishwashing rag); biodegradable soap; and a spice kit including salt and pepper, cooking oil in a plastic squeeze tube, any of your favorite cooking spices, an extra set of matches and other small odds and ends that might be required for specific meals.

These days, backpackers can buy a week's worth of light-weight, easy-to-prepare meals right from the average grocery store. Countless varieties of instant noodle dishes and rice dishes are available for a fraction of the cost of freeze-dried backpacking meals. I generally opt for these because they require, in the most extreme forms, only a little powdered milk, water and olive oil. Instant mashed potatoes are simple to prepare, as are instant hot cereals, instant coffee, instant soups, Ramen-style noodles, dried tortellini and so on. In addition, I carry dehydrated vegetables along with a few fresh goodies like a carrot or potato or two.

Naturally, the seemingly endless variety of dehydrated backpacking foods available these days allows for many options. For the most part these foods are well worth the price because most taste good, are easy to prepare and weigh next to nothing.

For breakfast, I usually opt for cold cereal, which can be removed from the box and placed in a zip-lock plastic bag. Dehydrated milk can be packed this way as well. Along with cereal I usually like dried fruit (apple slices, banana chips, apricot, etc.) for breakfast and for snacks. I rarely eat a regular sit-down lunch while hiking as I prefer the convenience of munching on snacks throughout the day (e.g. nuts, dried fruit, breakfast bars, granola bars).

Lastly, don't deny yourself the pleasure of sitting down to a trout dinner at 10,000 feet. Those lakes teeming with small brook trout are ideal places from which to harvest a few trout for dinner or breakfast. I like them just about any way they can be cooked, including fried and baked in foil. Include some wild onions, butter, pepper and whatever other seasonings you desire and you've created a gourmet meal.

Better still, at least in my opinion, is freshly killed grouse. Thus come autumn you're likely to find me packing a shotgun and a bird-hunting license. If you understand grouse habitat and habits (ruffed, blue and spruce grouse) you can invent hiking routes that take you through appropriate terrain in many of our wilderness areas. That, of course, is a subject for an entirely different book. Suffice it to say, however, that grouse cooked over a fire ranks amongst my favorite foods on the trail or on my patio grill.

Because dehydrated foods require water in their preparation I like to camp within reasonable proximity of a spring or mountain stream. I also carry two water bottles. On the trail you should drink water often to avoid dehydration. Much has been made about impure drinking water but I've never given a second thought to drinking from springs and tiny alpine streams high in the mountains and I've never had any kind of reaction to drinking this water.

The buzz word in recent times has been giardia and most people writing on the subject in outdoor magazines seem to go along with official sources who suggest boiling water for 15 or 20 minutes. These official sources have obviously never tried to boil water for 20 minutes on a Coleman Peak stove at 10,000 feet. In a few places I have read that giardia cases amongst alpine backpackers are nearly non-existent. My personal preference is to enjoy the water from cold, tumbling alpine streams and springs and not worry about the highly unlikely chance of harmful impurities. I don't drink water from lakes, creeks in lake basins, lower elevation streams or rivers unless I purify the water (by boiling, typically).

In any event, drink lots of water. Don't wait until you feel thirsty. Instead, make a point of taking a few swallows of water as often as possible, especially when you are laboring over rough, steep country.

Choosing a Campsite

The composition of the ideal campsite will undoubtedly vary from person to person but a few generalizations can certainly be made. Most of us, being anglers, like to camp near a lake or stream full of trout. I make a habit of staying well back from the shore so evidence of my stay won't mark the fragile ri-

Water emanating from alpine springs and from streams above timberline (and above lake basins) is generally safe to drink, not to mention superbly cold and refreshing.

During fall, bird hunters who understand grouse habitat can find these delectable fowl in many Western wilderness areas. Nothing beats a dinner of grouse and a breakfast of brook trout. Be sure to secure the appropriate license for the state you visit.

parian landscape.

I also like a little shelter so I look for proximity to timber. In addition, I like enough elevation so I can see what is around me and I look for the slightest of slopes to aid in draining rainwater should one of those sneaky alpine storms descend during the night. For the same reason—storms and the lightning that often accompanies them—I avoid cliffs, talus slides and ravines (rocks can bounce lightning around like a pingpong ball). Naturally, I won't set up camp in the middle of a fragile alpine meadow, although the edges of these meadows are certainly open game.

So what are we left with? My ideal campsite would probably be a bench elevated slightly above the lake I intend to fish. On that bench I would look for a small clearing amongst the trees so I could see the stars at night and so I wouldn't have to partake in the arduous task of removing evergreen pitch from my tent or sleeping bag. Some of my favorite campsites, in fact, sit amidst the trembling leaves of the beautiful quaking aspens that cloak much of the high country in the Rockies.

Despite my vision of the ideal campsite I often settle for less. I've slept on top of rocky peaks just for the view and I've slept on narrow shelves above alpine streams rushing through steep canyons. I've set up camp in the middle of monotonous lodgepole pine expanses and I've camped atop high saddles strung like a hammock between two jagged peaks.

During and after my stay I try to erase all signs of having camped on that site. After all, the next person to visit that spot is probably looking for the same pristine solitude that caught my eye. I dig a small bathroom hole at least 100 yards from camp.

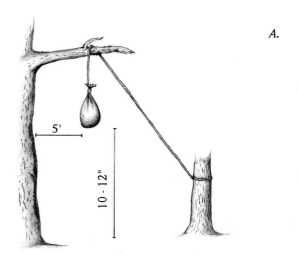

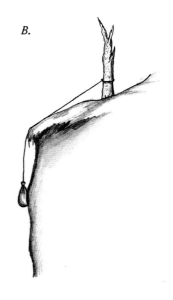

Suspending food away from the ground at night (and when you are fishing away from camp) will prevent bears and other raiding mammals from plundering your supply. In sparsely timbered areas, a cliff or large boulder can serve the same purpose (B).

When I leave, that hole is covered with the original dirt and duff layer and is then topped off with a big rock. The same hole is perfect for dumping waste water and meal leftovers. I remove any trash left by me and any left by those before me. For that purpose, I carry a medium-sized plastic kitchen-garbage bag.

Bear country, incidentally, deserves some special attention in setting up camp. Don't leave food in your pack or lying out in the open. Instead, hang all foodstuffs over a limb several feet away from the trunk of a tree. I carry 40 feet of duck cord for this purpose. After stowing the food in a large bag, I toss one end of the cord over an appropriate limb, tie that end to the grub bag and then hoist the whole works up toward the limb until it dangles a good 12 feet off the ground.

In grizzly country I make practice of cooking and eating well away from my intended campsite. In other words, if I intend to camp at a lake I will stop for a meal before I arrive. During an extended stay I simply walk to the other side or well down the shoreline to fix meals.

Grizzlies, despite their presence in some of our wilderness areas, are generally shy and rarely seen. Black bears are far more common and in some cases more of a pest to campers. Should one wander into camp looking for an easy meal you can generally frighten him or her away by yelling or banging pots together. Should that prove ineffective you might be better off just backing off until the bear has done what he decides to do, especially since black bear attacks have increased somewhat in recent years (which isn't surprising considering the number of people in the woods these days and the places where human habitation is springing up).

Sometimes other mammals can be more troublesome than bears, especially in popular areas. When I was a 13-year-old boy scout, my troop took a three day hiking trip into Idaho's Lemhi Mountains. The first night of the trip, my tent mate and I were awakened by scratching noises outside. We peered into the moonlit clearing where we had made camp only to see a pair of skunk tails protruding from the lower half of one fellow's backpack, which was leaning against a tree. Just at that moment another pair of skunks ran right past our front door intent on joining the feast. Eventually the scoutmaster woke up and shined a powerful flashlight beam onto the pack, frightening away the skunks.

When morning dawned we found that kid's backpack more or less shredded: He had left a bag with a half dozen juicy peaches in the pack, which was obviously more than a skunk could pass up.

On the Trail

Without question the easiest way to put a damper on a week-long wilderness trek is to overdo it the first day, at least if you are not used to backpacking at elevation. For that reason, I always use the first day of my first trip of the year as an adjustment period: A time to allow my system to adjust to the elevation, the weight of the pack, the feel of my boots.

In other words, I take it easy. I plan a route where I can cover four to six miles at a leisurely pace and then get in half a day or an evening of fishing. On subsequent days I'm a lot stronger from having eased into the trip than if I'd gone completely overboard on the first day.

I've never suffered from altitude sickness (Acute Mountain Sickness or AMS), but that's just luck of the draw: AMS can affect anybody, with level of physical conditioning a complete nonfactor.

In fact, supposedly as many as 25 or 30 percent of all people experience AMS symptoms at or above 10,000 feet. These symptoms include headaches, nausea, weakness and just plain feeling lousy (severe cases can progress to pulmonary edema, vomiting and loss of physical coordination).

The cure for AMS is simply to drop in altitude, at which point symptoms should subside after a time. In fact, AMS symptoms usually dissipate after a couple days even if the afflicted person just quits climbing any higher, but dropping back a thousand feet or more is the safest method. (Climbing higher is out of the question as doing so can heighten the symptoms and the severity of the sickness).

As mentioned previously, over-exertion can be a major problem on the trail for those not accustomed to carrying a heavy pack in steep, high-altitude terrain. Trail fatigue is only heightened by dehydration. So drink water often, before you feel thirsty. In addition, continue nibbling on snacks throughout the day; take steep terrain at a slow, deliberate pace; take short rest breaks as often as you like.

In many locales you may be faced with crossing talus slides

to reach certain remote waters. Talus can be dangerous, especially early in the season, just after snow melt. No matter what time of year, use an alternate course that takes you around talus whenever possible. When you have no choice, keep members of the group spaced apart so that any unfortunate mishap will not take everybody with it. Travel slowly and with great care using at least one of your hands on the rocks at all times. Above all, never trust a single rock. Even the largest, most stable-looking boulders might shift, slide or roll with the addition of your 200 pounds. So test each rock with one foot before plunging on top. Walk with your eyes, so to speak, by scanning ahead to plan your route carefully. You're not in a race, so take your time. The same philosophy holds true for fording mountain streams, although I suspect we fly anglers, simply due to experience, are better stream crossers than the average hiker.

When hiking cross-country, don't bother to blaze your route with plastic ribbon or with a knife blade: If you're map and compass skills can get you there they can certainly get you back. In one of my favorite wilderness areas, in fact, plastic ribbon blazes knotted around tree limbs seem to be popular these days. Anytime I find one, it comes off the tree and goes into my trash bag simply because those who tag the trees in this manner never seem to bother untagging them.

Dealing with Weather

The high mountains have their own weather: You might leave town on an 80- degree August day, hike into an alpine lake basin and get snowed on at 10,000 feet. Snow can indeed occur any time of year. Rain, meanwhile, should be expected. The Rockies are well known for their summer thunderstorms, which might span entire ranges like the Sawtooth's, Wind's or Absaroka's or might simply descend on your little alpine basin.

Either way you should be prepared for wet conditions because these thundershowers often occur with little warning. Sudden thunderstorms, the kind that leap suddenly from an otherwise perfect, postcard day generally issue forewarnings during the early to mid-afternoon. Big, puffy clouds start to build around the higher peaks and plateaus; intermittent winds blow, gaining strength as the afternoon passes; smoke from your fire spreads out through the tree canopy rather than rising into the skies; swallows and swifts fly lower and lower over the lake. These and other signs likely signal an oncoming storm.

Mountain storms can last mere minutes or for hours on end. Frequently, lightning is part of the package. Every year, several hundred Americans are zapped by lightning, most of these cases being avoidable with a little common sense. When high-mountain lightning storms occur, get away from the water and away from cliffs and rock outcroppings (and leave your fly rod behind as it can double as a dangerous lightning rod). Naturally, stay away from tall trees. If possible, take shelter amongst small, low lying trees; if caught in the open, drop to your knees and tuck your hands and head (don't lay flat on the ground). Also, separate members of a group. In short, just use your head and don't make a target of yourself.

Sudden weather changes are a fact of life in the high country, with afternoon thundershowers being commonplace during the summer months. Sometimes these thunderstorms descend on one peak or lake basin and other times they envelope entire ranges.

Rain storms in the mountains can douse you in no time and wet clothing is the surest way to invite hypothermia. Oddly enough, people usually experience hypothermia during reasonably good weather simply because once they've gotten wet and cold they assume the nice weather will warm them. Conversely, cases of hypothermia amongst cross-country skiers and snow shoers are rather uncommon simply because they are appropriately dressed.

The best way to deal with alpine weather is to go prepared for anything. I always pack an extra heavy shirt, jacket and thermal underwear along with a stocking cap. When I get cold, I warm myself immediately. When rain begins I dig out the raingear right away rather than wait, hoping the storm will pass quickly. If the weather seems to be settling in for a miserable few days I either pitch camp while the land is still dry or I make plans to return to the trailhead where I can figure out somewhere else to hike.

CHAPTER 9

Fishing Alpine Streams

With a lake full of golden trout waiting for me behind a steep 1,500-foot high hogback I set off on a cross-country course that would lead to what appeared to be the easiest route up the talus-covered slope. Part of my chosen course followed a stream that tumbled down the mountain before leveling in the basin below.

Following the stream through a dense stand of timber, I ran into a 50-foot precipice which curled the stream's pristine waters into a most elegant waterfall. I skirted left until I found a suitable place to scramble up the escarpment. Then I walked back toward the streambed where I found a large, deep pool quivering in a rock hollow immediately above the falls. When I approached the edge, trout scurried away everywhere.

Perhaps I didn't need to be in such a hurry to get to that golden trout lake after all. I strung a rod, tied on a No. 10 Elk Hair Caddis and caught brook trout after brook trout after brook trout. Most were six to 10 inches but a few reached a surprising 14 inches. I took the rest of the morning to cover the remaining 500 yards to the bottom of the ridge I had intended to climb.

Indeed, the alpine streams often hold suprisingly large concentrations of trout, with brook trout, cutthroat and rainbows (sometimes golden trout) all represented in one locale or another. What's more, only on very rare occasions will you need concern yourself with matching hatches because trout living in these alpine streams take just about anything that looks edible.

Learning where to find trout in the high-mountain streams warrants far more attention than matching your flies to the prevalent insect species. Naturally, the character of each stream will dictate where you should look for trout. Some alpine brooks meander through meadows looking for all the world like a small

Some alpine streams flow glassy smooth through alpine meadows and demand a quiet approach from fly anglers.

Many mountain streams are characterized by a continual series of riffles and pools.

spring creek. In these streams, where the water is perfectly clear by late summer, trout are exceptionally spooky and take cover at the slightest hint of danger.

Therefore, when you fish these meadow streams, stay low and use any available cover to approach trout. In fact, you should make every effort to locate individual trout rather than casting blindly in an effort to cover the water. Use 10- or 12-foot leaders so the splash from the fly line won't occur too close to the fish. If indeed you can avoid spooking them during the approach and the presentation, these trout from alpine meadow streams usually prove quite cooperative.

Effective dry flies for these flat-water situations include Parachute Adams or Gulper Specials, small Elk Hair Caddis, ants, small hoppers, beetles and Griffith's Gnats. If you can't tempt trout to the surface, try a small Pheasant Tail Nymph, Gold Ribbed Hare's Ear or Soft Hackle, or use a streamer.

Streamers for this kind of work are those that land with minimal splash and then sink quickly and easily. My favorites are the Mickey Finn, Bucktail Coachman and Spruce Matuka. Brook and cutthroat trout are especially susceptible to small streamers, so I generally opt for these flies instead of nymphs on the flat sections of alpine meadow streams.

Cast the streamer well above the trout allowing the fly an opportunity to sink and then retrieve with six to eight inch pulls across stream. You can also cast down-and-across to the trout and then simply pump the rod tip up and down as the fly swings across stream under tension from the current. Either way, trout from these small creeks generally try to beat the stuffing out of your streamer.

If you opt for nymphs, which can be highly productive, use two flies at a time and employ a dry fly as a strike indicator (an Elk Hair Caddis or a Royal Wulff). Space the two nymphs by eight to 10 inches.

Once in a while trout in these meadow sections can get turned on to a particular hatch, at which time they can feed rather selectively. Certain mayflies, along with caddisflies, can hatch in dense enough numbers to cause fairly selective feeding. On a spring creek at lower elevation, a heavy hatch might require you to match not only the color, size and shape of the natural, but also the particular stage of the insect's emergence on which the trout are keying (e.g. ascending nymph, surface film emerger, stillborn or adult).

Trout feeding on a heavy hatch in alpine streams rarely get this fussy. Just give them something of the right size and shape and nine times in 10 you fool them. For this reason I carry a variety of Gulper Specials to imitate mayflies and a variety of Elk Hair Caddis to mimic various caddis. In both cases I carry sizes 12-18. With caddis patterns, I tie some with an olive body and others with a tan body. I tie Gulper Specials with olive bodies and gray bodies. In neither case do I think body color makes much difference to alpine trout.

Even during a reasonably heavy hatch of mayflies or caddis, a flying ant pattern performs wonderfully so I never leave home without a couple dozen ants, most with black bodies and hackle-tip wings; a few with cinnamon bodies and wings.

More common than slow, meandering streams are those that tumble over the landscape. Even those creeks that flow gently through quiet meadows end up tumbling down a moun-

Other alpine streams rush violently over the landscape offering pocket water fishing to those willing to hop about on the rocks and fallen trees.

tain or through a ravine or canyon sooner or later. These fast-water sections are easy to fish so long as you remember that any fitting looking pocket, no matter how small, could very well hold a trout.

For that reason I like to work my way up such streams, casting (or dabbling) a fly into every little nook and cranny. I am constantly surprised by the size of trout that live in some of the tiny pockets on these little alpine streams.

Large dry flies designed to float high and dry are the ticket for this "pocket water" fishing. Amongst the best are foam-bodied hopper patterns, Royal Wulffs, Jugheads and large Elk Hair Caddis. All of these patterns float well enough that you can skate, jig and dabble them on the surface—an action that frequently proves irresistible even to a trout that passes on a dead-drift fly. By skating and dabbling the fly in these small pockets you allow the trout plenty of chance to see the fly. A dead-drift fly might drift through the trout's small window so fast that the fish either doesn't see it or it may drift fast enough that the fish instinctively realizes that his attack would invariably be too late anyway.

Thus the keys for fishing tumbling alpine streams are first to consider every small pocket to be trout water and then to keep the fly in the pocket for as long as possible.

Many sections of alpine streams fall somewhere in between the character of pocket water and flat water. These sections look like the average river or creek a lot of us grew up with: rock gardens and riffles, undercut banks, smooth runs, flat tailouts, funneling channels, boulders, overhanging willows, side channels, etc. Again, the rule to remember is that any piece of water that looks "trouty" should be the recipient of at least one cast.

In some places you might encounter beaver ponds. Treat these like miniature lakes that require a quiet approach. I often cast nymphs, retrieving them just as I would on a lake. Often the best approach on a beaver pond is to sneak up from below the dam so you can cast with little more than your upper torso visible to the trout in the pool above.

Because beaver ponds yield some surprisingly large trout I never pass one up. Once you get to high elevation, near and above timberline, however, you have by and large left the beaver behind. So look for ponds in the protected valleys and canyons well below the high crags.

As a general rule I always spend some time exploring the creeks that I encounter on my way into the high lakes. Some streams—namely those that dry up or freeze solid— will prove devoid of trout; others might yield only the tiniest of fish. Many of the alpine streams are teeming with trout that are eager and willing to grab a fly.

Selected Patterns for High Mountain Streams

Elk Hair Caddis (Al Troth)
Hook: Dry fly, No. 10-18 (Partridge #L3A)
Body: Dubbed fur, olive, brown or tan
Hackle: Grizzly or brown, palmered
Wing: Elk body hair

Black Flying Ant
Hook: Dry fly, No. 10-16 (Partridge #L4A)
Body: Two distinct balls of black fur
Wings: Hackle tips
Hackle: Two or three turns of black

Bob's Foam Hopper (Bob Roberts)
Hook: 3XL dry fly, No. 6-12 (Partridge #E1A)
Body: Closed-cell foam colored with waterproof pen (yellow, tan or pale olive)
Wing: Turkey quill sections
Legs: Two knotted sections of rubberleg material
Hackle: Light brown, short
Head: Continuation of foam body protruding in front of hackle

Mickey Finn
Hook: 4-5XL streamer, No. 6-12 (Partridge #D7A)
Body: Silver or gold tinsel or diamond braid
Wing: Bucktail or calftail, bottom to top as follows: yellow, red, yellow

Spruce Matuka
Hook: 3-4XL streamer, No. 6-10 (Partridge #D4A)
Body: Rear half red floss; front half peacock herl
Rib: Fine gold oval or wire
Wing: Two dark furnace saddles tied matuka style
Collar: Dark furnace saddle hackle

Royal Wulff (Lee Wulff)
Hook: Dry fly, No. 10-16, 2XL (Partridge #E1A)
Tail: Moose hair or elk hock
Body: Three parts: peacock herl, red floss, peacock herl
Rib: Fine wire, counterwrapped
Wings: White calftail or calf body, divided
Hackle: Brown

Gulper Special (Al Troth)
Hook: Dry fly, No. 12-18 (Partridge #L3A)
Tail: Grizzly hackle fibers
Body: Olive, cream or gray dubbing
Wing: White poly yarn
Hackle: Grizzly, parachute style

Foam Beetle
Hook: Dry fly, No. 12-14 (Partridge #L3A)
Body: Peacock herl
Legs: Two to three turns of black hackle
Shellback: Black or gray foam
Head: Continuation of shellback

Bucktail Coachman
Hook: 4-5XL streamer, No. 6-12 (Partridge #D4A)
Tail: golden pheasant tippets
Body: Peacock herl
Rib: Fine gold wire, counterwrapped
Wing: White bucktail or calftail
Throat: Soft brown hackle fibers

CHAPTER 10

Western Wilderness Areas: An Angler's Guide

In this chapter you will find state-by-state listings of the various Western wilderness areas that offer the best alpine-lake fishing. Under each heading, I list reference maps. In many cases these maps are not suitable for cross-country travel: The national forest maps are usually non topographical (no contour lines) and many of the wilderness area maps are of a rather small scale (1:63,360 or 1:100,000). So use these maps in the planning stages of your trips but purchase USGS 7.5 Minute topos for actual wilderness travel.

WYOMING

Bridger Wilderness
Fitzpatrick Wilderness
Popo Agie Wilderness
Location: Wind River Mountains, Shoshone and Bridger-Teton National Forests, west-central Wyoming
Acreage: Bridger Wilderness: 428,169
Fitzpatrick Wilderness: 198,525
Popo Agie Wilderness: 101,870
Fishable Lakes: Hundreds (more than 200 in the Bridger Wilderness alone)
Major Stream Systems: Green River, Popo Agie River
Reference Maps: Bridger-Teton National Forest, Pinedale Ranger District and Bridger Wilderness
Scale: 1:126,720
Shoshone National Forest, South Half
Information & Maps: Shoshone National Forest
Wind River Ranger District
Masonic Bldg.
P.O. Box 186
Dubois, WY 82513
307-455-2466

(Fitzpatrick Wilderness)

Shoshone National Forest
Lander Ranger District
Hwy. 287 West
Lander, WY 82520
307-332-5460
(Popo Agie Wilderness)

Bridger-Teton National Forest
Pinedale Ranger District
210 W. Pine Street
Pinedale, WY 82941
307-367-4326
(Bridger Wilderness)

Wyoming Game and Fish Department
District Office
117 South Sublette Ave.
Pinedale, WY 82941
307-733-2321

Grayling caught in the Bridger Wilderness, Wyoming.

Bridger Wilderness, Wyoming.

Notes: Undoubtedly, these three wilderness areas in Wyoming offer the finest golden trout fishing available today. Large golden trout—12-18 inches—are not uncommon for those anglers willing to put in long miles in the higher elevations of the Wind River Range. The Bridger-Teton National Forest (Pinedale office) offers a brochure telling which lakes in the Bridger Wilderness hold trout (and grayling)—this is a valuable guide for those looking for particular species like goldens or grayling. Also, with Bridger being the most popular (because it is most accessible) of the three wilderness areas, anglers willing to work at it, can find total isolation alongside splendid fishing in the Fitzpatrick and Popo Agie Wilderness Area's.

Jedediah Smith Wilderness and Winegar Hole Wilderness
Location: Western Wyoming near the Teton Mountains
Acreage: Jedediah Smith: 123,451
    Winegar Hole: 10,715
Fishable Lakes: approx. 12
Reference Maps: Jedediah Smith and Winegar Hole Wildernesses Targhee National Forest
    Scale: 1:63,360
Information & Maps: Targhee National Forest
    Supervisor's Office
    P.O. Box 208
    St. Anthony, ID 83445
    208-624-3151

Teton Basin Ranger District
Driggs, Idaho 83422
208-354-2312

Wyoming Game and Fish Department
Box 67
Jackson, WY 83001
Note: Two fish limit on cutthroat in the Snake River Drainage.

Teton Wilderness Area and Gros Ventre Wilderness Area
Location: Northwest Wyoming: Teton Wilderness is immediately south of Yellowstone National Park; Gros Ventre Wilderness is immediately southeast of Teton National Park
Acreage: Teton Wilderness: 585,238
    Gros Ventre Wilderness: 287,000
Fishable Lakes: approx. 65
Major Stream Systems: Teton Wilderness— Yellowstone River; Buffalo Fork; Pacific Creek; Gros Ventre Wilderness—Gros Ventre River; Crystal Creek; Granite Creek
Reference Maps: Bridger-Teton National Forest
    Buffalo and Jackson Ranger Districts
    Scale: 1:126,720
Information & Maps: Bridger-Teton National Forest
    Jackson Ranger District
    140 E. Broadway
    P.O. Box 1689
    Jackson, WY 83001

307-733-4755
Bridger-Teton National Forest
Buffalo Ranger District
Highway 287
P.O. Box 278
Moran, WY 83013
307-543-2386

Wyoming Game and Fish Department
Box 67
Jackson, WY 83001

Notes: Two fish limit on cutthroat in the Snake River Drainage.

Snowy Range, Medicine Bow National Forest
Location: South-central Wyoming, Medicine Bow National Forest

Information & Maps: Medicine Bow National Forest
    2468 Jackson Street
    Laramie, WY 82070
    307-745-8971

Wyoming Game and Fish Dept.
Region 5
528 S. Adams
Laramie, WY 82070

Notes: The Snowy Range area, part of the Medicine Bow Mountains, features several dozen high-mountain lakes, some drive-in, others hike-in, located east of the town of Saratoga.

IDAHO

Sawtooth Wilderness Area

Location: Sawtooth National Recreation Area, central Idaho
Acreage: 217,000
Fishable Lakes: approx. 200
Major Stream Systems: South Fork Payette River; North Fork Boise River; Middle Fork Boise River
Reference Maps: Sawtooth National Forest Fairfield and Ketchum Ranger Districts
Information & Maps: Sawtooth National Recreation Area Headquarters
Star Route (Hwy 75)
Ketchum, ID 83340
208-726-8291

Stanley Ranger Station
Stanley, Idaho 83278
208-726-8291

Boise National Forest
1750 Front Street
Boise, ID 83702
208-334-1516

Boise National Forest
Lowman Ranger District
Lowman, ID 83637
208-259-3361

Idaho Department of Fish and Game
Region 4

868 East Main
Jerome, ID 83338
208-324-4350

Notes: The Sawtooth Wilderness is part of the 754,000-acre Sawtooth National Recreation Area. East of the Sawtooth Wilderness Area, across the Sawtooth Valley, rise the White Cloud Peaks which offer dozens of hike-in alpine lakes. South of the White Cloud Peaks lie the Boulder Mountains and farther to the east, the Pioneer Mountains. Both of these ranges also hide many hike-in, high-elevation lakes.

Frank Church River of No Return Wilderness

Location: Encompasses a huge portion of central Idaho
Acreage: 2.3 million
Fishable Lakes: hundreds
Major Stream Drainages: Salmon River and its numerous tributaries
Maps: Frank Church-River of No Return Wilderness, North Half
Frank Church-River of No Return Wilderness, South Half
(Forest Service)
Scale: 1:100,000
Challis National Forest
Payette National Forest
Salmon National Forest
Information & Maps: Salmon National Forest
Highway 93 North
Salmon, ID 83467
208-756-2215
Challis National Forest

P.O. Box 404
Challis, ID 83226
208-879-2285

Payette National Forest
P.O. Box 1026
McCall, ID 83638
208-634-8151

Bitterroot National Forest
Nez Perce National Forest
Grangeville, ID 83530
208-983-1950

Idaho Department of Fish and Game
Salmon Office
P.O. Box 1336
Salmon, ID 83467
208-756-2271

Notes: The River of No Return Wilderness, spanning 2.3 million acres, is by far the largest wilderness area in the lower 48 states. The area is so vast that those willing to cover a lot of trail miles can experience a kind of total solitude virtually unattainable in many of our other wilderness areas.

Gospel Hump Wilderness

Location: Nez Perce National Forest of Central Idaho
Acreage: 203,473
Fishable Lakes: approx. 20
Reference Maps: Nez Perce National Forest Payette National Forest
Information & Maps: Nez Perce National Forest

Golden Trout, White Cloud Peak Range, Idaho

Alpine Angler

Grangeville, ID 83530
208-983-1950

Idaho Department of Fish and
Game
Region 2
Lewiston, ID 83501
208-799-5010

Selway-Bitterroot Wilderness
Location: North-central Idaho, with the
eastern edge of the wilderness
area spanning into Montana;
including parts of four national
forests
Acreage: 1,337,910
Fishable Lakes:more then 200
Major Stream Systems: Selway River and
its many tributaries, including
Moose Creek; Lochsa River's
southern tributaries
Reference Maps: Selway-Bitterroot
Wilderness
(Forest Service)
Scale: 1:100,000
Bitterroot National Forest
Nez Perce National Forest
Clearwater National Forest
Lolo National Forest
Information & Maps: Bitterroot National
Forest
1801 North First Street
Hamilton, MT 59840
406-363-3131

Nez Perce National Forest
Grangeville, ID 83530
208-983-1950

Nez Perce National Forest
Selway Ranger District
Kooskia, ID 83539
208-926-4258

Clearwater National Forest
12730 Hwy. 12
Orofino, ID 83544
208-476-4541

Lolo National Forest
Bldg. 24A, Ft. Missoula
Missoula, MT 59801
406-329-3814

Idaho Department of Fish
and Game
1540 Warner Avenue
Lewiston, ID 83501
208-799-5010

Montana Department of Fish
Wildlife and Parks
Region 2
3201 Spurgin Rd.
Missoula, MT 59801
406-542-5500
Notes: If you visit the border region of the

Sawtooth Wilderness, Idaho

Selway-Bitterroot Wilderness, bear in mind
that you need fishing licenses from both
Idaho and Montana if you intend to fish
lakes on both sides.

Hells Canyon Wilderness
Location: Western Idaho, along the Snake
River
Fishable Lakes: Approximately 20
Reference Maps: Nez Perce National Forest
Information & Maps: Nez Perce National
Forest
Supervisor's Office
Grangeville, ID 83530
208-983-1950

Idaho Department of Fish and
Game
Region 4
868 East Main
Jerome, ID 83338
208-324-4350

MONTANA

Bob Marshall, Great Bear, and
Scapegoat Wilderness Complex
Location: Northwest Montana, spanning
from the southern boundary of
Glacier National Park (Great
Bear Wilderness) all the way to
the mountains northeast of
Missoula; includes parts of four
national forests
Acreage: Bob Marshall: 1,009,356
Great Bear: 286,700
Scapegoat: 239,936
Fishable Lakes: More than 50

Major Stream Systems: South Fork
Flathead River, Middle Fork
Flathead River, West Fork Sun
River, Blackfoot River, and
numerous major tributaries to
these rivers
Reference Maps: Bob Marshall, Great
Bear, and Scapegoat Wilderness
Complex
(Flathead, Helena, Lewis and
Clark, and Lolo National
Forests)
Information & Maps: Flathead National
Forest
1935 Third Avenue East
Kalispell, MT 59901
406-755-5401

Helena National Forest
301 South Park, Rm. 334
Drawer 10014
Helena, MT 59626
406-449-5201

Lewis and Clark National Forest
1101 15th Street North
Great Falls, MT 59403
406-791-7700

Lolo National Forest
Bldg. 24, Fort Missoula
Missoula, MT 59801
406-329-3750

Montana Department of Fish,
Wildlife and Parks
1420 East Sixth Avenue,
Helena, MT 59620
Kalispell Office: 406-752-5501

Missoula Office: 406-542-5500
Notes: This huge wilderness complex—
especially the massive Bob Marshall
Wilderness Area—offers excellent
opportunity to find solitude and to find
seldom-fished high lakes.

Absaroka-Beartooth Wilderness Area
Location: Southwest Montana, bordering
　　　　on the northeast edge of
　　　　Yellowstone National Park
Acreage: 924,465
Fishable Lakes: Hundreds
Major Stream Systems: Boulder River,
　　　　Hellroaring Creek, Buffalo
　　　　Creek, Stillwater River, Slough
　　　　Creek
Reference Maps: Absaroka Beartooth
　　　　Wilderness
　　　　(Custer, Gallatin and Shoshone
　　　　National Forests)
　　　　Scale: 1:100,000
Information & Maps: Custer National
　　　　Forest
　　　　Beartooth Ranger District
　　　　Rt. 2 Box 3420
　　　　Red Lodge, MT 59068

　　　　Gallatin National Forest
　　　　Livingston Ranger District
　　　　Rte. 62, Box 3197
　　　　406-222-1892

　　　　Shoshone National Forest
　　　　Clarks Fork Ranger District
　　　　P.O. Box 1023
　　　　Powell, WY 82435

Absaroka-Beartooth Wilderness, Montana.

Montana Department of Fish,
Wildlife and Parks
1420 East Sixth Avenue
Helena, MT 59620
Notes: The southernmost tip of the
Absaroka-Beartooth Wilderness lies within
the state of Wyoming, thus requiring
anlgers hiking into that region to possess a
Wyoming fishing license. In addition to the
20-some lakes inside this Wyoming corner
of the wilderness, the Wyoming end of the
Beartooth Plateau, which lies outside the
wilderness boundary, offers about two
dozen hike-in lakes. Throughout, the
Absaroka-Beartooth Wilderness is
comparatively under-utilized by fly anglers
despite the countless lakes and numerous
streams.

Lee Metcalf Wilderness Area
Location: Southwest Montana, northwest
　　　　of Yellowstone National Park
Acreage: 250,297
Fishable Lakes: More than 100
Major Stream Systems: numerous
　　　　tributaries to the Madison and
　　　　Gallatin Rivers, including the
　　　　West Fork of the Gallatin River
Reference Maps: Lee Metcalf Wilderness
　　　　Area
　　　　(Beaverhead and Gallatin
　　　　National Forests)
　　　　Scale: 1:63,360 (1 inch = 1
　　　　mile)
Information & Maps: Beaverhead National
　　　　Forest
　　　　Madison Ranger District
　　　　5 Forest Service Rd.
　　　　Ennis, MT 59729
　　　　406-682-4253

　　　　Gallatin National Forest
　　　　Federal Building
　　　　P.O. Box 130
　　　　Bozeman, MT 59771
　　　　406-587-4701

　　　　Montana Department of Fish,
　　　　Wildlife and Parks
　　　　1420 East Sixth Ave.
　　　　Helena, MT 59620

Anaconda Pintler Wilderness Area
Location: Southwest Montana, southwest
　　　　of the town of Anaconda
Acreage: 158,656
Fishable Lakes: Approximately 60
Major Stream Systems: East Fork Bitterroot
　　　　River, Pintler Creek, La Marche
　　　　Creek, Seymour Creek
Reference Maps: Anaconda Pintler
　　　　Wilderness
　　　　(Beaverhead, Bitterroot and
　　　　Deerlodge National Forests)
　　　　Scale: 1:50,000
Information & Maps: Beaverhead National

Bitterroot Mountains, Montana.

Absaroka-Beartooth Wilderness, Montana.

Forest
420 Barrett Street
Dillon, MT 59725
406-683-3900

Deerlodge National Forest
Federal Bldg., P.O. Box 400
Butte, MT 59703
406-496-3400

Bitterroot National Forest
1801 North First Street
Hamilton, MT 59840
406-363-3131

Mission Mountains Wilderness Area and Mission Mountains Tribal Wilderness
Location: Western Montana, north of
Missoula in the Mission
Mountains
Acreage: Mission Mountains Wilderness:
91,778
Fishable Lakes: Approximately
100 combined
Major Stream Systems: Jocko River, Swan
River, Crazy Horse Creek, Elk
Creek
Reference Maps: Mission Mountains
and Mission Mountains Tribal
Wildernesses
Flathead National Forest
Scale: 1:50,000
Information & Maps: Flathead National
Forest
1935 Third Ave., E.
Kalispell, MT 59901

406-755-5401

Confederated Salish and
Kootenai Tribes
P.O. Box 370
Bigfork, MT 59911
406-675-2700

Montana Department of Fish,
Wildlife and Parks
490 North Meridian
P.O. Box 67
Kalispell, MT 59901
406-752-5501
Note: Tribal Recreation permit and fishing
stamp required to fish Reservation waters
(available at stores on the reservation.).

Cabinet Mountains Wilderness Area
Location: Northwestern Montana, south of
the town of Libby
Acreage: 94,360
Fishable Lakes: Approximately 60
Major Stream Systems: East Fork Bull
River, Swamp Creek
Reference Maps: Cabinet Mountains
Wilderness
Kootenai and Kaniksu National
Forests
Scale: 1:63,360 (1 inch = 1 mile)
Information & Maps: Kootenai National
Forest
506 U.S. Hwy. 2 West
Libby, MT 59923
406-293-6211
Montana Department of Fish,
Wildlife and Parks

490 North Meridian
P.O. Box 67
Kalispell, MT 59901
406-752-5501

Rattlesnake Wilderness Area
Location: Lolo National Forest, western
Montana
Acreage: 33,000
Fishable Lakes: Approximately 30
Reference Maps: Lolo National Forest
Principal and Boise Meridians
Information & Maps: Lolo National Forest
Bldg. 24, Fort Missoula
Missoula, MT 59801
406-329-3750

Montana Department of Fish,
Wildlife and Parks
490 North Meridian
P.O. Box 67
Kalispell, MT 59901
406-752-5501

Flint Creek Range
Location: Deerlodge National Forest,
north of Anaconda
Reference Map: Deerlodge National Forest
Information & maps: Deerlodge National
Forest
P.O. Box 400
Butte, MT 59703
406-496-3400

Montana Department of Fish,
Wildlife and Parks

Flat Tops Wilderness, Colorado.

1420 East Sixth Avenue
Helena, MT 59620
Notes: Though not a wilderness area, the Flint Creek Range features some 50 or more hike-in trout lakes

COLORADO

Flat Tops Wilderness
Location: White River National Forest, northwest Colorado
Acreage: 235,035
Fishable Lakes: Approximately 75
Major Stream Systems: White River, South and North Forks
Reference Maps: White River National Forest
Information & Maps: White River National Forest
P.O. Box 948, 9th and Grand
Glenwood Springs, CO 81602
303-945-2521

Colorado Division of Wildlife
6060 Broadway
Denver, CO 80216
303-297-1192

Maroon Bells-Snowmass Wilderness, Eagles Nest Wilderness, Hunter-Frying Pan Wilderness, Collegiate Peaks Wilderness, Holy Cross Wilderness, Mt. Massive Wilderness, Raggeds Wilderness
Location: White River and San Isabel National Forests, west-central Colorado
Acreage: Maroon Bells-Snowmass: 19,194
Eagles Nest: 132,906
Hunter-Frying Pan: 82,729
Collegiate Peaks: 166,716
Holy Cross: 122,388
Mt. Massive: 27,980
Raggeds: 64,928
Fishable Lakes: More than 100 between the various wilderness areas
Reference Maps: White River National Forest
San Isabel National Forest
Information & Maps: White River National Forest
P.O. Box 948, 9th and Grand
Glenwood Springs, CO 81602
303-945-2521

San Isabel National Forest
1920 Valley Drive
Pueblo, CO 81008
719-545-8737

Colorado Division of Wildlife
6060 Broadway
Denver, CO 80216
303-297-1192

Mount Zirkel Wilderness
Location: Routt National Forest, north of Steamboat Springs in northern Colorado
Acreage: 160,568
Fishable Lakes: Approximately 50
Reference Maps: Routt National Forest
Information & Maps: Routt National Forest
29587 West Hwy. 40, Ste. 20
Steamboat Springs, CO 80487
303-879-1722

Colorado Division of Wildlife
6060 Broadway

Denver, CO 80216
303-297-1192

Indian Peaks Wilderness
Rawah Wilderness
Comanche Peak Wilderness
Location: North and south of Rocky Mountain National Park, northern Colorado
Acreage: Indian Peaks: 70,374
Rawah: 73,068
Comanche Peak: 66,791
Fishable Lakes: Indian Peaks Wilderness: Approx. 30
Rawah /Comanche Peaks Wildernesses: Approx. 25
Reference Maps: Arapaho and Roosevelt National Forests
Information & Maps: Arapaho and Roosevelt National Forests
240 West Prospect Rd.
Fort Collins, CO 80526
303-498-1100

Colorado Division of Wildlife
6060 Broadway
Denver, CO 80216
303-297-1192

South San Juan Wilderness
Weminuche Wilderness
Sangre De Cristo Range
Location: Rio Grande and San Juan National Forests, southern Colorado
Acreage: South San Juan: 158,790
Weminuche: 487,704
Fishable Lakes: South San Juan Wilderness: Approx. 10
Weminuche Wilderness: Approx. 75

Sangre De Cristo Range:
Approx. 30
Reference Maps: San Juan National Forest
Rio Grande National Forest
Information & Maps: San Juan National
Forest
701 Camino Del Rio, Room 301
Durango, CO 81301
303-247-4874

Rio Grande National Forest
1802 West US Hwy. 160
Monte Vista, CO 81144
719-852-5941

Colorado Division of Wildlife
6060 Broadway
Denver, CO 80216
303-297-1192

Grand Mesa Area
Location: Grand Mesa National Forest east
of Grand Junction, Colorado
Fishable Lakes: Approximately 50
Reference Maps: Grand Mesa National
Forest
Information & Maps: Grand Mesa National
Forest
Forest Headquarters
2250 Hwy. 50
Delta, CO 81416
303-874-7691

White River National Forest
P.O. Box 948, 9th and Grand
Glenwood Springs, CO 81602
303-945-2521

Colorado Division of Wildlife
6060 Broadway
Denver, CO 80216
303-297-1192
Notes: This area is not a wilderness, but travel restrictions are in effect for motorized vehicles so

Columbine, Flat Tops Wilderness, Colorado.

many hike-in lakes and lake basins are available for backpacking anglers.

Rocky Mountain National Park
Location: Northern Colorado
Fishable Lakes: 42
Reference Maps: Arapaho and Roosevelt
National Forests
Information & Maps: Rocky Mountain
National Park
Estes Park, CO 80517
Notes: Waters within Rocky Mountain National Park contain one or more of four different species of trout: cutthroat, brook, rainbow and browns. Prior to 1970, non-native trout, including Yellowstone cutthroat, were planted in park waters. Since then, however, the park waters have been stocked with native Colorado River cutthroat and greenback cutthroat in an effort to restore the fisheries to their original condition. A Colorado angling license is required to fish within the park and some of the lakes—including some backcountry waters—are closed to fishing. The park can send you information detailing the opportunities and regulations regarding the park's waters. Incidentally, the greenback cutthroat trout has been listed as a threatened species and thus when caught in waters open to fishing, they must be immediately released unharmed.

NEVADA

Ruby Mountains and East Humbolt Range
Location: Northeast Nevada, Humbolt
National Forest
Reference Maps: Humbolt National Forest,
Ruby Mountains Ranger District
(Intermountain Region, USDA

Humbolt National Forest, Nevada.

Hoover Wilderness, California. Ken Hanley photo.

Forest Service)
Information & Maps: Ruby Mountains
Ranger District
P.O. Box 246
Wells, NV 89835
702-752-3357
Notes: Information provided by the Humbolt National Forest, Ruby Mountains Ranger District lists the following lakes as fishable waters within the Ruby Mountains and East Humbolt Range:

Lake	Elevation	Acres	Depth (feet)	Fish Species
Hidden #1	9,500	6.1	32	cutthroat
Hidden #2	9,500	2.8	9	cutthroat
Boulder	9,500	10.5	10.5	brook trout
Cold #1	9,900	3.7	28	brook trout
Cold #2	9,900	1.8	24	brook trout
Echo	9,820	29	155	brook trout
Grey's	8,600	4.9	15	cutthroat
Favre	9,500	19	45	brook trout
Island	9,800	7.5	22	brook trout
Lamoille	9,700	13.6	20	brook trout
Liberty	9,700	21	108	brook and lake trout
Robinson	9,000	17.4	4.5	brook trout
Steele	9,500	10	48	brook trout
Verdi	10,150	6	86	cutthroat
Angel	8,400	13	29	rainbow, brook, tiger trout
Overland	9,000	15	?	brook trout
Smith	9,100	4	?	stocked; status unknown

Nevada Department of Wildlife
Region II Headquarters
1375 Mt. City Hwy.
Elko, NV 89801
702-738-5332
Notes: The state of Nevada, while not exactly abounding with alpine lakes, does offer the least-utilized wilderness areas in America. Until 1989, the 64,667-acre Jarbridge Wilderness Area was Nevada's only designated wilderness. However, the Nevada Wilderness Protection Act of 1989 set aside an additional 13 wilderness areas totaling more than 733,000 acres. Countless streams, some of them offering excellent trout fishing, drain these wilderness areas all of which are little appreciated by anyone other than those who live in sparsely populated northern Nevada and south-central Idaho. The Ruby Mountain Range and nearby East Humbolt Range feature most of the state's alpine lakes.

Fishing licenses should be obtained by mail if possible because, as of this writing, only three towns across northern Nevada had license agents.

CALIFORNIA

Trinity Alps Wilderness
Location: Shasta and Trinity National
     Forests, Northern California
Acreage: 513,100
Fishable Lakes: More than 50
Major Stream Systems: North Fork Trinity
     River
Reference Maps: Trinity Alps Wilderness
     (Forest Service)
     Shasta and Trinity National
     Forests
     (USDA-Forest Service)
Information & Maps: Shasta-Trinity
     National Forests
     2400 Washington Ave.
     Redding, CA 96001
     916-246-5222

Lassen Peak National Park
Caribou Wilderness
Thousand Lakes Wilderness
Location: Lassen National Forest, northern
     California
Acreage: Caribou: 20,500
     Thousand Lakes: 16,300
Fishable Lakes: Combined more than 100
Major Stream Systems: Warner Creek, Lost
     Creek, Manzanita Creek,
     Sulpher Creek
Reference Maps: Lassen National Forest
     (USDA Forest Service)
Information & Maps: Lassen National Forest
     55 South Sacramento Street
     Susanville, CA 96130
     916-257-2151

Desolation Wilderness
Location: Just southwest of Lake Tahoe in
     Eldorado National Forest
Acreage: 63,500
Fishable Lakes: Approximately 75
Major Stream Systems: Rubicon River
Reference Maps: Desolation Wilderness
     (Forest Service)
     Eldorado National Forest
     (USDA Forest Service)
Information & Maps: Eldorado National
     Forest
     100 Forni Road
     Placerville, CA 95667
     916-644-6048

Mokelumne Wilderness
Carson-Iceberg Wilderness
Location: South of Lake Tahoe, central
     California Sierras
Acreage: Mokelumne: 100,600
     Carson-Iceberg: 158,900
Fishable Lakes: More than 20 combined
Major Stream Systems: Stanislaus River
Reference Maps: Mokelumne Wilderness
     (Forest Service)

Yosemite National Park. Ken Hanley photo.

Carson-Iceberg Wilderness
(forest service)
Stanislaus National Forest
Toiyabe National Forest
Eldorado National Forest
Information & Maps: Stanislaus National
Forest
19777 Greenley Rd.,
Sonora, CA 95370
209-532-3671

Eldorado National Forest
100 Forni Road
Placerville, CA 95667
916-644-6048

Toiyabe National Forest
1200 Franklin Way
Sparks, NV 89431
702-355-5301

Emigrant Wilderness
Location: Stanislaus National Forest,
immediately north of Yosemite
National Park
Acreage: 112,300
Fishable Lakes: Approximately 80
Major Streams: South Fork Stanislaus
River, Cherry Creek
Reference Maps: Emigrant Wilderness
(USDA Forest Service)
Stanislaus National Forest
(USDA Forest Service)
Information & Maps: Stanislaus National
Forest
19777 Greenley Rd.,
Sonora, CA 95370
209-532-3671

Note: Yosemite National Park also offers many
alpine lakes. Check park regulations.

Sequoia and Kings National Parks
John Muir Wilderness
Ansel Adams Wilderness
Hoover Wilderness
Golden Trout Wilderness
Monarch Wilderness
Jennie Lakes Wilderness
Kaiser Wilderness
Location: This huge complex of
wilderness areas and two
national parks comprise a
majority of the central-California
Sierra Nevada Range, including
the Kern River drainage, which
is the historic home of golden
trout.

Acreage: John Muir Wilderness:
581,000
Ansel Adams Wilderness:
230,300
Hoover Wilderness:
48,600
Golden Trout Wilderness:
303,300
Monarch Wilderness: 44,900

Hoover Wilderness, California. Ken Hanley photo.

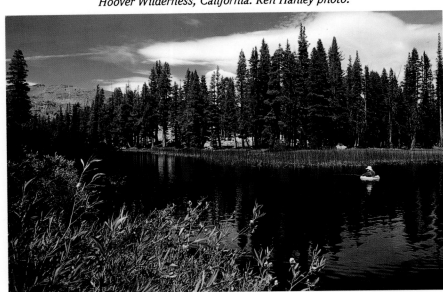

High Uintas Wilderness, Utah.

wherein these lovely trout evolved. Two subspecies of golden trout are presently recognized: the South Fork Kern golden trout *(Salmo aguabonita aguabonita),* native to the upper portions of the South Fork Kern River and to Golden Trout Creek and the Volcano Creek (Little Kern) golden trout *(Salmo aguabonita whitei),* which is native to the Little Kern River and several of its tributaries.

For more than 100 years, golden trout have been stocked—by official and unofficial laborers—into various lakes and streams throughout much of the High Sierra. Presently, golden trout are found in some 300 lakes and 700 miles of stream in California. Between 1928 and 1937, California golden trout were sent to several other states, including Wyoming, Montana, Utah, Colorado and Washington. Wyoming now sustains the largest golden trout-rearing operation of these states and also offers the world's foremost opportunity to find large golden trout. In 1939, the California Legislature prohibited exportation of golden trout eggs or fry.

A booklet titled, *Golden Trout Of The High Sierra,* produced and distributed by the California Department of Fish and Game, lists waters known to contain golden trout. To receive this booklet, contact California Fish and Game. The information in the booklet may be somewhat dated and should thus be cross-referenced with Ralph Cutter's *Sierra Trout Guide* (Frank Amato Publications) and by calling California Fish and Game about specific waters.

OREGON

Eagle Cap Wilderness

Location: Wallowa Mountains, northeast
  Oregon, Wallowa-Whitman
  National Forest
Acreage: 293,735
Fishable Lakes: Approximately 75
Major Stream Systems: Minam River,
  Lostine River, Wallowa River,
  Imnaha River
Reference Maps: Eagle Cap Wilderness
  (Forest Service)
  Scale: 1:63,360
  Wallowa-Whitman National
  Forest, North Half
Information & Maps: Wallowa-Whitman
  National Forest
  Eagle Cap Ranger District
  Enterprise, Oregon 97828
  503-426-3104
  Wallowa Whitman National
  Forest
  Wallowa Valley Ranger Station
  Joseph, Oregon 97846
  503-423-2171

  Wallowa Whitman National

Jennie Lakes Wilderness: 10,300
Kaiser Wilderness: 22,700
Fishable Lakes: Hundreds
Major Stream Systems: Many, including
  the Kings River, San Joaquin
  River, Roaring River, Kern River,
  Little Kern River and Kaweah
  River
Reference Maps: "Topographic Map of the
  John Muir Wilderness And The
  Sequoia-Kings Canyon National
  Parks Backcountry" (a 3-map set
  available from USDA Forest
  Service)

Hoover Wilderness
Ansel Adams Wilderness
Golden Trout-South Sierra
Wildernesses
Kaiser Wilderness
Monarch Jennie Lakes
Wildernesses
(all USDA-Forest Service)
Information/Maps: Inyo National Forest
  873 North Main Street
  Bishop, CA 93514

619-873-5841

Sierra National Forest
1600 Tollhouse Road
Clovis, CA 93612
209-487-5155

Sequoia National Forest
900 West Grand Avenue
Porterville, CA 93257
209-784-1500

Sequoia and Kings Canyon
National Parks
Chief Ranger Office
Three Rivers, CA 93271
209-565-3341

Notes: Given the state's huge population, it's no wonder that the wilderness areas of the Sierras are heavily used. Still, like anywhere else, those willing to work the hardest can enjoy solitude in the backcountry. What's more, the Sierra is home to golden trout and the Golden Trout Wilderness south of Sequoia National Park features the watersheds

Eagle Cap Wilderness, Oregon.

Forest Headquarters
P.O. Box 907
Baker, OR 97814
503-523-6391

Oregon Department of Fish and
Wildlife
Northeast Regional Office
Rt. 2, Box 2283
La Grande, OR 97850
503-963-2138

Notes: Fishing in Oregon, by Dan Casali
and Madelynne Diness covers many of the
lakes within the Eagle Cap Wilderness.
This book is available at most sporting
goods stores and book stores around the
state.

Three Sisters Wilderness, Oregon.

Mt. Jefferson Wilderness
Location: Central Oregon Cascades,
    Willamette National Forest
Acreage: 100,208
Fishable Lakes: Approximately 65
Major Stream Systems: Upper North
    Santiam River, South Fork
    Breitenbush River
Reference Maps: Mt. Jefferson Wilderness
    (National Forest)
    Scale: 1:63,360

Willamette National Forest
Information & Maps: Willamette National
    Forest
    Detroit Ranger District

Star Route Box 320
Mill City, OR 97360
503-854-3366

Deschutes National Forest
Sisters Ranger District
Sisters, OR 97759

Willamette National Forest
Headquarters
P.O. Box 10607
Eugene, OR 97401

Oregon Department of Fish and
Wildlife
Northwest Region
Rt. 5, Box 325
Corvallis, OR 97330
503-757-4186

Notes: Fishing in Oregon, by Dan Casali
and Madelynne Diness covers many of the
lakes within the Mt. Jefferson Wilderness.
This book is available at most sporting
goods stores and book stores around the
state.

Three Sisters Wilderness Area
Location: Central Oregon Cascades,
    Willamette and Deschutes
    National Forests
Acreage: 242,400
Fishable Lakes: More than 100
Major Stream Systems: Upper South Fork,
    McKenzie River; Separation
    Creek
Reference Maps: Three Sisters Wilderness
    Map
    (Forest Service)
    Scale: 1:100,000
    Willamette National Forest map
    Deschutes National Forest map
Maps & Information: Deschutes National
    Forest
    211 NE Revere Street
    Bend, OR 97701

Deschutes National Forest
Sisters Ranger District
Sisters, OR 97759

Willamette National Forest
P.O. Box 10607
Eugene Federal Building
Eugene, OR 97440

Willamette National Forest
McKenzie Ranger District
McKenzie Bridge, OR 97401

Oregon Department of Fish and
Wildlife
Central Region
61374 Parrell Rd
Bend, OR 97702
503-388-6363

Notes: Fishing in Oregon, by Dan Casali
and Madelynne Diness covers many of the

lakes within the Three Sisters Wilderness. This book is available at most sporting goods stores and book stores around the state.

Waldo Lake Wilderness Area
Location: Central Oregon Cascades, Willamette National Forest
Acreage: 37,162
Fishable Lakes: Approximately 30
Major Stream Systems: Upper North Fork of Middle Fork of the Willamette River; Fisher Creek
Reference Maps: Waldo Lake Wilderness and Recreation Area map (Forest Service)

Willamette National Forest Map
Maps & Information: Willamette National Forest
P.O. Box 10607
Eugene, OR 97440

Willamette National Forest
Oakridge Ranger District
46375 Hwy. 58
Westfir, OR 97492
Notes: Fishing in Oregon, by Dan Casali and Madelynne Diness covers many of the lakes within the Waldo Lake Wilderness. This book is available at most sporting goods stores and book stores around the state.

Sky Lakes Wilderness Area
Location: Due south of Crater Lake National Park in southern Oregon; Rogue River and Winema National Forests
Acreage: 113,590
Fishable Lakes: Approximately 50
Major Stream Systems: Middle Fork Rogue River
Reference Maps: Sky Lakes Wilderness (Forest Service)
Rogue River National Forest

Shooting Stars, Mt. Jefferson Wilderness, Oregon.

Winema National Forest
Information & Maps: Rogue River National Forest
P.O. Box 520
Medford, OR 97501
503-776-3600

Rogue River National Forest
Butte Falls Ranger Station
P.O. Box 227
Butte Falls, OR 97522

Winema National Forest
P.O. Box 1390
Klammath Falls, OR 97601
503-883-6714

Oregon Department of Fish and Wildlife
Southwest Region
3140 NE Stephens
Roseburg, OR 97470
503-440-3353
Notes: Fishing in Oregon, by Dan Casali and Madelynne Diness covers many of the lakes within the Sky Lakes Wilderness. This book is available at most sporting goods stores and book stores around the state.

Mountain Lakes Wilderness
Location: Winema National Forest, southern Oregon
Acreage: 23,071
Fishable Lakes: Approximately 10
Reference Maps: Mountain Lakes Wilderness (map suitable for cross-country travel) (Forest Service)

Winema National Forest
Information & Maps: Winema National Forest
Klammath Ranger District
1936 California Avenue
Klammath Falls, OR 97601

Oregon Department of Fish and Wildlife
Southeast Regional Office
Box 8
Hines, OR 97738
Notes: Fishing in Oregon, by Dan Casali and Madelynne Diness covers many of the lakes within the Mountain Lakes Wilderness. This book is available at most sporting goods stores and book stores around the state.

UTAH

High Uintas Wilderness
Location: Uintas Mountains, northeastern Utah
Acreage: 456,704
Fishable Lakes: More than 250
Major Stream Systems: Upper Bear River,

Lupine, Mt. Jefferson Wilderness, Oregon.

Rock Creek, Lake Forks River, Black's Fork River, Yellowstone Creek, Uintas River, Smith Fork River, Henry's Fork River, Beaver Creek
Reference Maps: High Uintas Wilderness (map suitable for cross-country travel) (Forest Service)
Ashley National Forest
Wasatch-Cache National Forest
Information & Maps: Wasatch National Forest
8226 Federal Building
125 South State Street
Salt Lake City, UT 84111

Naturalist Basin Area
Kamas Ranger District
P.O. Box 68
Kamas, UT 84036
801-783-4338

Bear River and Black's Fork Drainages
Bear River Ranger Station
P.O. Box 1880
Evanston, Wyoming 82930
801-642-6662

Smith's Fork and Henry's Fork Drainages
Mountain View Ranger District
Lone Tree Rd., Hwy. 44
Mountain View, Wyoming 82939
307-782-6555

Ashley National Forest
1680 W. Highway 40
Vernal, UT 84078

Rock Creek and North Fork Duchesne Drainages
Duchesne Ranger District
85 W. Main, P.O. Box 1
Duchesne, UT 84021
801-738-2482

Lake Fork, Yellowstone and Uinta Drainages
Roosevelt Ranger District
West Hwy. 40, P.O. Box 338
Roosevelt, UT 84066
801-722-5018
State of Utah Natural Resources
Division of Wildlife Resources

Northeast Regional Office
152 East 100 North
Vernal, UT 84078
801-789-3103

Division of Wildlife Resources
Main Office
1596 West North Temple
Salt Lake City, UT 84116
801-538-4700

Notes: The Utah Division of Wildlife Resources publishes a series of 10 booklets that list each and every fishable lake in and around the High Uintas Wilderness. For a nominal fee, you can order these directly from the department and indeed anyone planning to fish the High Uintas should not be without this valuable information. The publications are each titled *Lakes of the High Uintas* and are broken down by drainage as follows:

Publication #	Drainage
83-6	Duchesne Drainage
81-6	Ashley Creek Drainage
86-9	Sheep Creek, Carter Creek and Burnt Fork Drainages
83-6	Provo and Weber River Drainages
85-7	Bear River and Black's Fork Drainages
86-10	Smith's Fork, Henry's Fork and Beaver Creek Drainages
87-6	Whiterocks River Drainage
85-8	Rock Creek Drainage
82-7	Dry Gulch and Uinta River Drainages
83-5	Yellowstone, Lake Fork and Swift Creek Drainages

The Utah Division of Wildlife Resources has, in the past, stocked California golden trout in a handful of lakes within the High Uintas Wilderness; their current status, as of this writing in 1994, is unknown. Arctic grayling are available in several lakes. Otherwise, brook trout and cutthroat, along with a few rainbows, are common in the wilderness lakes. Very rare amongst Western lakes are those above 10,000 feet that sustain native trout populations. At least one lake in the High Uintas—Lower Ottoson Lake—apparently does indeed harbor native cutthroat at an elevation of 11,075 feet!

Boulder Mountain Area and Escalante Mountains
Location: Dixie National Forest, southern Utah (Escalante and Teasdale Ranger Districts)
Fishable Lakes: Several dozen, including some drive-in lakes
Reference Map: Dixie National Forest Powell, Escalante and Teasdale

High Uintas Wilderness, Utah.

Ranger Districts
Information & Maps: Dixie National Forest
Escalante Ranger District
270 West Main
P.O. Box 246
Escalante, UT 84726
801-826-4221

Dixie National Forest
Teasdale Ranger District
P.O. Box 99
Teasdale, UT 84773

Utah Division of Wildlife Resources
Southern Regional Office
622 North Main Street
Cedar City, UT 84720
801-586-2455

WASHINGTON

Goat Rocks Wilderness and William O. Douglas Wilderness
Location: Gifford-Pinchot National Forest, southern Washington Cascades
Acreage: Goat Rocks Wilderness:
105,600 acres
William O. Douglas Wilderness:
166,000
Fishable Lakes: Approximately 50
Major Stream Systems: Cispus River, Tieton River, Cowlitz River tributaries
Reference Maps: Goat Rocks Wilderness (National Forest)
Scale: 1:63,360

William O. Douglas and Norse Peak Wilderness Areas (National Forest)
Scale: 1:63,360

Gifford-Pinchot National Forest Pacific Crest National Scenic Trail, Washington Southern Portion
(USDA Forest Service, Pacific Northwest Region)
Information & Maps: Gifford-Pinchot National Forest
500 West 12th Street
Vancouver, WA 98660
206-696-7500

Wenatchee National Forest
P.O. Box 811
Wenatchee, WA 98801
509-662-4335

Washington Department of Wildlife
600 Capitol Way N.
Olympia, WA 98501-1091
206-753-5700

Glacier Peak Wilderness
Location: Northeast of Seattle in the northern Washington Cascades
Acreage: 576,865 acres
Fishable Lakes: Approximately 65
Major Stream Systems: White River, Suiattle River, Napeequa River, Agnes Creek
Reference Maps: The Glacier Peak Wilderness
(Mt. Baker-Snoqualmie National Forest)
Scale: 1:100,000

Mt. Baker-Snoqualmie National Forest

Pacific Crest Scenic Trail, Washington Northern Portion
(USDA Forest Service, Pacific Northwest Region)
Information & Maps: Mt. Baker-Snoqualmie National Forest
1018 First Avenue
Seattle, WA 98104
206-442-0170

Washington Department of Wildlife
600 Capitol Way N.
Olympia, WA 98501-1091
206-753-5700

The Pasayten Wilderness
Location: Okanogan National Forest, northern Washington Cascades
Acreage: 530,000
Fishable Lakes: More than 50
Major Stream Systems: Chewack River, Lost River, Pasayten River
Reference Maps: The Pasayten Wilderness (Okanogan National Forest)
Scale: 1:100,000

Okanogan National Forest

Pacific Crest Scenic Trail,
Washington Northern Portion
(USDA Forest Service, Pacific
Northwest Region)
Information & Maps:Okanogan National
Forest
P.O. Box 950
Okanogan, WA 98840
509-422-2704

Washington Department of
Wildlife
600 Capitol Way N.
Olympia, WA 98501-1091
206-753-5700

Lake Chelan-Sawtooth Wilderness
Location: Okanogan and Wenatchee
National Forests, northern
Washington Cascades
Acreage: 146,000
Fishable Lakes: Approximately 20
Reference Maps: Okanogan National Forest
Wenatche National Forest
Information & Maps: Okanogan National
Forest
P.O. Box 950
Okanogan, WA 98840
509-422-2704

Wenatchee National Forest
P.O. Box 811
Wenatchee, WA 98801
509-662-4335

Washington Department of
Wildlife
600 Capitol Way N.
Olympia, WA 98501-1091
206-753-5700

Alpine Lakes Wilderness and Henry M. Jackson Wilderness
Location: Mt. Baker-Snoqualmie National
Forest, central Washington
Cascades
Acreage: Alpine Lakes Wilderness:
393,360
Henry M. Jackson:103,591
Fishable Lakes: Alpine Lakes Wilderness:
Approx. 100
Henry M. Jackson Wilderness:
Approx. 20
Major Stream Systems: North Fork
Skykomish River (Henry M.
Jackson Wilderness)
Middle Fork Snoqualmie River
(Alpine Lakes Wilderness)
Reference Maps: Henry M. Jackson
Wilderness Area
(National Forest) Mt. Baker-
Snoqualmie National Forest
Wenatchee National Forest

Alpine Lakes Wilderness, Washington

Pacific Crest Scenic Trail,
Washington Northern Portion
(USDA Forest Service, Pacific
Northwest Region)
Information & Maps: Mt. Baker-
Snoqualmie National Forest
1018 First Avenue
Seattle, WA 98104
206-442-0170

Wenatchee National Forest
P.O. Box 811
Wenatchee, WA 98801
509-662-4335

Washington Department of
Wildlife
600 Capitol Way N.
Olympia, WA 98501-1091
206-753-5700

Clearwater Wilderness and Norse Peak Wilderness
Location: Mt. Baker-Snoqualmie National
Forest, Washington Cascades
Acreage: Clearwater Wilderness:14,374
Norse Peak Wilderness: 51,000
Fishable Lakes: Clearwater Wilderness:
Approx. 8
Norse Peak Wilderness: Approx. 8
Reference Maps: William O. Douglas and
Norse Peak Wilderness Areas
(Forest Service)
Mt. Baker-Snoqualmie National
Forest
White River Ranger District Map
Mt. Baker-Snoqualmie National
Forest

Pacific Crest National Scenic
Trail, Washington Southern
Portion
(USDA Forest Service, Pacific
Northwest Region)
Information & Maps: Mt. Baker-Snoqualmie
National Forest
1018 First Avenue
Seattle, WA 98104

206-442-0170

Washington Department of
Wildlife
600 Capitol Way N.
Olympia, WA 98501-1091
206-753-5700

Mt. Baker Wilderness
Location: Mt. Baker and surrounding area,
northern Washington Cascades
Acreage: 117,600
Fishable Lakes: Approximately 20
Reference Maps: Mt. Baker-Snoqualmie
National Forest
Information & Maps: Mt. Baker-
Snoqualmie National Forest
1018 First Avenue
Seattle, WA 98104
206-442-0170

Washington Department of
Wildlife
600 Capitol Way N.
Olympia, WA 98501-1091
206-753-5700

Indian Heaven Wilderness
Location: Gifford-Pinchot National Forest,
southern Washington Cascades
Acreage: 20,600
Fishable Lakes: Approximately 30
Reference Maps: Indian Heaven-Trapper
Creek Wilderness Areas
(Forest Service)
Gifford Pinchot National Forest
Pacific Crest National Scenic
Trail, Washington Southern
Portion
(USDA Forest Service, Pacific
Northwest Region)
Information & Maps: Washington
Department of Wildlife
600 Capitol Way N.
Olympia, WA 98501-1091
206-753-5700

Photo by DeAnn Montgomery

LEARN MORE ABOUT FLY FISHING AND FLY TYING WITH THESE BOOKS

If you are unable to find the books shown below at your local book store
or fly shop you can order direct from the publisher below.

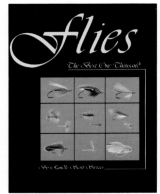

Flies: The Best One Thousand
Randy Stetzer
$24.95 (HB: $34.95)

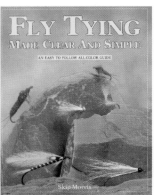

Fly Tying Made Clear and Simple
Skip Morris
$19.95 (HB: $29.95)

The Art of Tying the Dry Fly
Skip Morris
$29.95 (HB:$39.95)

Curtis Creek Manifesto
Sheridan Anderson
$6.95

American Fly Tying Manual
Dave Hughes
$9.95

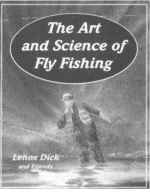

The Art and Science of Fly Fishing
Lenox Dick
$19.95

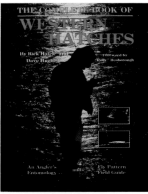

Western Hatches
Dave Hughes, Rick Hafele
$24.95

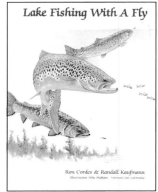

Lake Fishing with a Fly
Ron Cordes, Randall Kaufmann
$26.95

Advanced Fly Fishing for Steelhead
Deke Meyer
$24.95

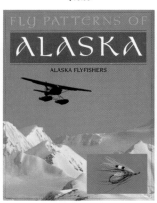

Fly Patterns of Alaska
Alaska Flyfishers
$19.95

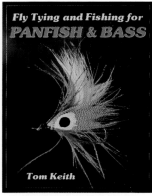

Fly Tying & Fishing for Panfish and Bass
Tom Keith
$19.95

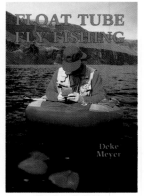

Float Tube Fly Fishing
Deke Meyer
$11.95

VISA, MASTERCARD or AMERICAN EXPRESS ORDERS CALL TOLL FREE: 1-800-541-9498
(9-5 Pacific Standard Time)

Or Send Check or money order to:

Frank Amato Publications
Box 82112
Portland, Oregon 97282

(Please add $3.00 for shipping and handling)